Enlightenment Unleashed

*How Your Pet Can Lead
You to Spiritual Transformation*

Margaret Meloni, PhD

Copyright ©2023 Margaret Meloni

All rights reserved. No part of this publication may be reproduced, distributed, or transmitted in any form or by any means, including photocopying, recording, or other electronic or mechanical methods, without the prior written permission of the publisher, except in the case of brief quotations embodied in reviews and certain other non-commercial uses permitted by copyright law.

www.margaretmeloni.com

ISBN paperback: 978-1-7329075-3-9

ISBN eBook: 978-1-7329075-4-6

Dedication

From Alex to Zeke and all who were in between.

May you and your animal friends be well. May you be happy. May you be at ease. And may you be free from suffering.

Table of Contents

Dedication iii

Abbreviations ix

Introduction 1

Chapter 1: Our Pets Are Family 5
    Animals Tell Our Story 8
    We Pay Their Way 14
    How Did We Get Here? 18
    Interspecies Family 21
    End Notes 25

Chapter 2: Animals in Early Buddhism 27
    Introduction to the Jātaka Tales 28
    Animals in the Jātaka Tales 32
    Animal Jātakas and Their Themes 36
    What Is the Message? 42
    The Importance of the Jātaka Tales 47
    How Is this Relevant Today? 49
    End Notes 54

Chapter 3: Animal Rebirth 56
    About the Animal Realm 60
    Is There No Escape? 68
    End Notes 76

Chapter 4: Animals Appearing in *Suttas* 77
    Animals and the Rules of Conduct 78
    Suttas: A Broader Context 81
    Elephants, Deer, Lions, and Jackals 89
    Animal Welfare and Vegetarianism 92
    An Imperfect World 99

End Notes 101

Chapter 5: Animals in Other Buddhist Cultures 102
  The Journey to the West 103
  Rats in Bhutan 106
  On Symbolism 109
  Going to the Dogs 113
  Cross-Cultural Connections 115
  End Notes 119

Chapter 6: Love Them and Let Them Go 121
  Cemeteries and Burials 122
  Prayers and Memorials 123
  Cloning? Please Don't 126
  Let Your Practice Inform Your Choice 129
  This Is Personal 130
  End Notes 133

Chapter 7: Animals to the Rescue 134
  Pet Therapy 137
  Horses Can Help Us 140
  Prison Programs 143
  Cat Videos Rule the Internet 146
  End Notes 148

Chapter 8: Your Responsibility 149
  PETS Act 150
  Be Aware and Be Prepared 153
  Adopt with Care 156
  Remember: They Are Animals 162
  Euthanasia 165
  Karma 167
  End Notes 169

Chapter 9: More Pets, More Attachment 171
The Truth of Suffering 173
Transferring Attachment to Pets 175
Aversion to Humans? 178
Skillful Attachment 181
Plenty of Practice 184
End Notes 186

Chapter 10: Our Pets and Our Practice 187
Alex the Aging Coach 188
Alex, Soho, Maple, and *Dukkha* 190
Perfect Teachers? 191
Now It Is Up To You 195
End Notes 197

Conclusion 198

Bibliography 203

Abbreviations

These are the abbreviations used for the Pāli Buddhist Texts which may be quoted throughout this book.

AN	Aṅguttara Nikāya
Dhp	Dhammapada
DN	Dīgha Nikāya
Jat	Jātaka
MN	Majjhima Nikāya
SN	Saṃyutta Nikāya
Sn	Sutta Nipāta
Thag	Theragāthā
Ud	Udāna
Iti	Itivuttaka

Introduction

One day, a member of the group I meditated with said to me, "You write and talk about when a friend or family member dies, but what about when we lose our pets?" She had recently lost a cat who had been by her side for nineteen years. This loss was deep and painful. I carried her question with me and contemplated how best to write about grieving our animal friends. Around the same time, another friend told me they thought it would be interesting if my next book was about the spiritual nature of our pets. This, too, was a compelling idea.

I began to realize that I did not have anything new to add to the topic of grieving our pets. If I wrote something, I would most likely be recycling my thoughts around how Buddhism can help us with death and grief. For me, the teachings that helped with the death of family and friends were also helpful when it came time to say goodbye to pets because at some point, many of us have stopped looking at our pets as animals, and we have elevated them to a place where we might even hold them in higher regard than the people around us.

As I looked around and saw this happening, I knew what I had to do. It was my job to remind all of us that animals are not our children or our partners. I was ready to say, "Hey, everyone! Come to your senses. Pets are not people!"

But as I spent more time thinking about our relationships with our pets and what that means to our Buddhist practice, I saw that perhaps I was the one who needed to come to her senses.

Who was I to lecture others about saying they had fur babies? I know that coming home to two cats after my closest family members died helped to keep me sane. There were times when all I wanted was to close the door and be alone. But I was not alone. I had two furry companions near me at all times.

Recalling how much I relied on my cats also opened my mind to some wisdom. The first was something Venerable Karma Lekshe Tsomo said to me when I interviewed her for the *Death Dhamma Podcast*. She reminded me that we need to meet people where they are. And the other, a saying that I use all too frequently, is this is how it is.

As I thought about what type of topics to include in a book about our pets and our Buddhist practice, I had a mini epiphany. In the West, we have evolved in such a way that the role of pets in our social structure has changed. This is nothing for me to be judgmental about. It does not require my attention. Nobody is waiting for me to tell them what kind of relationship to have with their pets. People think of pets as family. This is how it is. If I want to help us on our path and discuss the role our pets play in our practice, then I need to work with things how they are, meeting myself, and everyone else, exactly where we are.

Once that became clear, it was time to move forward. To find a way to combine how we live with our pets with an understanding of the role animals have played in Buddhist teachings so that we can best live with them, love them, and help one another live with more peace and less suffering.

It is true that pets are not people. But they can be your cherished companions and spiritual teachers.

In writing this book, I have used two terms that may spark some curiosity. The first is the word *animal*. Yes, human beings are animals, but I use the term *animal* in reference to our pets and other non-human animals.

I also use the term *owner*—as in *pet owner*. I mean no disrespect to our animal friends. I have adopted this as a conventional term to designate a human who has a pet who is dependent on them for care.

Thank you for your kind understanding.

Margaret Meloni

Chapter 1

Our Pets Are Family

Years ago, I worked with a husband-and-wife team. After about two years of marriage, they adopted a cute little cocker spaniel puppy. If I recall correctly, they named her Lily. She was so sweet and so loved. Each day, one or both of them regaled us with stories about Lily. As is true with many new pet owners, it was obvious to them that Lily was the smartest, best behaved, prettiest dog ever. When they asked me to care for Lily while they took a short trip, I knew they trusted me above all others. All went well, and they returned to a healthy, happy dog.

When I say this was years ago, I mean back before smartphones (gasp! Yes, it is true) and also before digital cameras. Once upon a time, we could not take pictures and create videos with our phones, and cameras used film that had to be developed. Despite the effort to take and develop photographs, this couple took many pictures of Lily. And these were not just regular photographs of a dog doing tricks or playing. These were carefully arranged, artistic photos of Lily posing in hats, glasses, and outfits, always against backdrops that was either beautifully draped, in theme, or both. In this era, dog clothing and fashion accessories were not as prevalent as today. Some of Lily's outfits were doll clothes or baby clothes, and some were designed and constructed for Lily by her human parents. I can only imagine the time, effort, and money that went into these pictures. It was clear that Lily was the star of this household.

That was the first time I observed a pet transcending the role of an animal sidekick to one of kinship. This trend has steadily grown—and pets have transitioned from being mere animals to becoming beloved family members.

It's not that my friends, family, and I did not love the animals who shared our home. It is just that there was a time when the boundaries were different. We had a cat named Puddi. He lived to be seventeen years old. That was significant at that time because he lived outdoors and moved with us across the country and to three different houses. Because my parents adopted Puddi before they adopted either of their two children, we used to joke that he was their test case. If all had not gone well with Puddi, my brother and I would have been left at the orphanage. This weak attempt at humor never really implied that Puddi was their first baby or that he was our older sibling.

Somewhere along the way, our relationship with our pets has blossomed into deeper friendships and inclusion in family photos and events. Dogs, cats, and other animal friends figure prominently in holiday cards. Sometimes, the picture of the furry friend *is* the holiday card. I have seen pictures of dogs and cats participating in weddings. Just before New Year's Eve last year, I saw more than one person post about looking forward to staying home and celebrating with their dog or their cat. On

Mother's Day and Father's Day, I see posts about fur babies and about pets as children.

> What about you? What is your relationship like with your animal friend? If you named your best friend, would the answer be a human or a completely different animal?

Think about your own relationships with your pets as we consider:

- How human and pet relationships have evolved.
- How pets became family members.
- How we benefit from our human-pet relationships.
- What Buddhism teaches us about our human-pet relationships.

There was a time when Lily and other pets would not have taken on such a leading role. Approximately twelve to fourteen thousand years ago, if Lily had existed, she would have been a wolf cub. Her primary role would have been to help hunt for food.

In an early example of the bond between dogs and people, a Paleolithic tomb found in Northern Israel included a human buried with a dog. The hand of the human appears to have been placed on the dog's shoulder.[1]

About eight thousand years ago, nomadic people settled in the Fertile Crescent, in what is now Western Asia and Northern Africa. These settlements attracted rodents, and rodents attracted cats. Although originally only royalty kept pets—cats by the ancient Egyptians and lap dogs by early Chinese emperors—as cats and dogs continued to live alongside villagers, the villagers came to accept them as part of the group.[2]

In Europe, pet keeping became an accepted practice at the end of the seventeenth century among the wealthy and nobility and then in the late eighteen century among the middle classes. It is most likely that the type of human-pet relationship that we see today came from nineteenth-century Victorian attitudes—specifically, that the human-pet relationship was a normal link with the natural world.[3] And now here we are. Sometimes a pet is a status symbol, especially if you own a purebred dog or a horse with a noble pedigree. Some animals provide security or pest control, but mostly they are our companions.

Just as Lily became the star of her family, pets have also taken the spotlight in our collective stories. From the early days of cinema to today's digital era, animals have played captivating roles on screens big and small. These roles help us to gain a deeper understanding of why our pets are such a significant part of our lives.

Animals Tell Our Story

Animals are an essential part of our story. Sometimes they take the lead. Sometimes they are a trusted sidekick or a confidant. The role of our animal companions has evolved along with our craft of storytelling. A quick look into the evolution of cinema, television, and social media provides insight.

The Kinetoscope, an early film-viewing device, became available in the 1890s, and short animal stories quickly followed, including *Skipping Dogs* in 1895 and *The Boxing Kangaroo* in 1896. One of the most popular shorts was *Rescued by Rover*, starring a collie named Blair who rescues a kidnapped baby. Dogs quickly became the most popular animal stars. But they were also joined by chimpanzees, monkeys, and others. There was Queenie the horse, Pepper the cat, and Anna May the elephant.[4]

In 1928, an actor named Emil Jannings was the first male lead to win an Academy award. There was another actor who received more votes, another leading male who would have won the award, if only he had been a human being: Rin Tin Tin, the famous German shepherd. Discovered during WWI in a burned-out dog kennel, Rin Tin Tin, his mother, and his siblings were rescued by an American soldier, US Air Corporal Lee Duncan, who brought them back to camp. Eventually, he brought Rin Tin Tin back to the United States, where he was discovered at a dog show and soon became one of Warner Brothers' biggest stars.[5] At one time, eighteen trained stand-ins alleviated stress from the original actor. By 1926, he was earning $6,000 per week, which was more than other human actors (and more than most people make today). His legacy lived on in his offspring.[6]

Throughout the years many animals have appeared in leading roles, and several shows have been built around the personality of a wise and wonderful animal lead. You might have heard of Lassie, the brave farm dog who always watched over his human companion Timmy. And there was Flipper, a dolphin who communicated with his adopted humans using whistles and clicks, and Mister Ed, the famous talking horse. In some ways through these characters, we see a recognition of our interconnectedness. A dog, a dolphin, and a sarcastic horse form bonds with humans in order to protect other beings and the environment. Various episodes of *Lassie* teach how to deal with grief, illness, and financial hardship. I would not say that these stories are meant to represent Buddhist values, but I would say that they show modern examples of using animals to teach us how to live ethically and harmoniously. The very creation of these stories shows that we were ready for deeper connections with our animal friends. Although *Lassie*, *Flipper*, and *Mister Ed* aired in the 1950s and 1960s, they continue to live in pop culture.[7]

In the 1960s and 1970s, animal shows took on more dimension. Documentaries became popular. There was *Mutual of Omaha's Wild Kingdom* and the *Undersea World of Jacque Cousteau*. The movie *Born Free* was released in 1966 and told the true story of husband-and-wife team George and Joy Adamson. The Adamsons lived in Kenya and saved a young lion cub, Elsa, who they raised until she was ready to live in the wild. In the movie, Elsa had her own cubs, and she brought them back to meet the Adamsons.

The Incredible Journey (1963) is the story of two dogs and a cat who travel three hundred miles through the Canadian wilderness to find their way home. In this story, we see the animals as friends, supporting and showing compassion toward one another. We also see them in real peril, foraging and hunting for food. There is this combination of animals showing human traits and animals being animals. In *Benji* (1974), we have the fictional account of an independent little dog who saves the two human children he loves from kidnappers.

In 1969, Scooby-Doo, the Great Dane who helps solve mysteries, was born. Scooby-Doo is an animal companion, detective, and lovable friend. He often walks on two legs, and he can talk. When he speaks, he sounds part dog, part human, as if he is manipulating his barks into words.

The 1990s were rife with movies about kids, and animals and their adventures. There were two movies about talking pigs, *Babe* and *Gordy,* and many movies about dogs. There was also a seal named Andre, a chimpanzee named Dunston, and a parrot named Paulie. Some attribute the number of animal movies to the fact that technology had improved and it was easier to make it look like a live animal was talking. Additionally, some of these movies were less expensive to make and had high profit margins as movie goers enjoyed the antics of all of these wise-cracking anthropomorphized critters.

The introduction of computer-generated imagery (CGI) allowed for the creation of more realistic animal characters, such as the dinosaurs in *Jurassic Park* (1993) and the animals in *The Lion King* (1994). *The Lion King* musical is still on tour at this time, and a new movie is scheduled for release in 2024.

In 2020, while in lockdown, the popularity of the Netflix show *Tiger King* led to at least one arrest for animal cruelty—a reminder that we might tolerate humans misbehaving toward one another but not toward our animal companions.[8]

We have crafted stories of resilience, friendship, drama, horror, and comedy, but we have not reserved the leading roles or significant plot points for humans. We have brought our animal companions along for the ride. Afraid to swim in the ocean? You can thank Shark Week, *The Meg* (2018), or even *Jaws* (1975). Not sure if it is safe to go into the woods? Well, *Cocaine Bear* (2023) is not going to make you feel better. But if you want to consider how forming a respectful bond with an animal can help you with your introspection and healing, then consider the documentary *My Octopus Teacher* (2020).

Current-day Buddhism has not escaped the allure of animals in our lives. I have been charmed by the fictional series *The Dalai Lama's Cat* by David Michie. Each book stars a cat who was rescued by His Holiness himself and who listens in as the Dalai Lama teaches others. Each story teaches Tibetan Buddhist wisdom through the life and adventures of this special feline. And the cat begins to contemplate these teachings and seeks to live their own life following the wisdom of their owner.

When not streaming movies or series or reading stories, we might be on social media. Do you know who owns the internet? Cats! OK, well, they do not exactly own the internet, but consider these facts:

- The first cat video was uploaded to YouTube in 2005.[9]
- In 2006, the first cat video went viral.[10]
- In 2015, cats drove an estimated 15 percent of all internet traffic.
- In 2020, searches for "cat" topped 50 million monthly on Google—an increase from 30 million searches per month in 2015.

- In August 2022, there were about 6.5 billion (yes, billion) cat pictures on the internet.[11]

While cat videos and pictures may dominate, there are also entire social media accounts built around pets' perceived or invented personalities. A look at popular pet accounts today shows dogs in the top two spots when measured by Instagram followers.

In terms of popularity at home, in 2022, dogs were the most popular household pets, with an estimated 69 million households owning a dog. Next were cats, with approximately 45.3 million homes; in third place were freshwater fish, with 11.8 million households. Birds came next, followed by small animals such as hamsters, rabbits, mice, and ferrets.[12]

If cats, dogs, fish, and birds are not your thing, do not be discouraged. You can also watch livestreams of monkeys, ponies, and all kinds of critters. I love watching the "bear cam," a live feed of Alaskan brown bears.

According to one survey, 35 percent of us have more photos of our pets on our phones than of our children or partners.[13] In a separate study, a look at a targeted group of two thousand dog and cat owners revealed that only 27 percent of them had more photos of their children than their pets, and 16 percent said they had more pictures of their partners than their pets. Research also revealed that survey participants take over four hundred images of their pets yearly.[14]

When you consider how pets have been anthropomorphized in popular culture, you can see how we might lean in the direction of animals. We see them talking, singing karaoke, and holding down jobs. TikTok videos have turned racoons, squirrels, parrots, turtles, spider monkeys, and others into media stars. We have been conditioned to love animals and to think of them as more and more like us. [15]

While animals may have captivated us on screens, their impact has transcended the fictional world. For many, the love we feel for our pets extends to the investments we make in their well-being.

We Pay Their Way

We spend good money keeping our pets healthy and photogenic. I often remark that I spend more money on veterinarian visits for my cats than on my own healthcare. And it would appear that I am not alone. I have heard friends discuss hip and back surgery for their dogs that cost $20,000 or more. I once had to decide whether to send a cat for radiation, and for a brief period, I took two chubby cats for regular weigh-ins as part of their weight loss program.

> What about you? How much time and money do you spend taking care of your furry, feathered or scaly companion? Do you place their needs above your own?

A Forbes Advisor report indicates that in 2020 we spent an average of $326 on veterinary care for our dogs or cats. Most dog owners spend from $500 to $1,999 annually on food, grooming, veterinary care, toys, dog walkers or sitters, and other items. [16]

Whether it is on clothing, grooming, birthday parties, or treats, who spends the most money on their pets? Pet owners in the United States come first: in 2021, US pet owners spent approximately $109 billion on their pets. This accounts for 53 percent of the worldwide pet care market. If we look at this in terms of per capita spending, the United States spends about $150 per person on their pets. The UK comes next at $93 per person. Other countries in the top five include France, Switzerland, and Germany. Japan is the highest-spending Asian country at just under $50 per person. Other countries spend too. In 2020, China's estimated pet spending was $31.89 billion. In the expanding Latin American pet market, Brazil stands out with the highest number of pets. Global expectations predict the pet clothing market to reach a value of at least $7 billion by 2028.[17]

Age and location also factor into your willingness to spend on your pet. Members of Gen Z (eighteen- to twenty-five-year-olds) are most likely to buy their dog a birthday cake or unique clothing or take the dog for training classes.[18]

Are you a New Yorker? If so, you might be part of the 40 percent who have spent more money on spoiling your dog than on satisfying your significant other (ouch). You might also belong to the group who spend more money on your dog's medical bill than on your own.[19]

Californians are likely to buy their dogs a Starbucks Puppuccino or order them a meal from a restaurant. Dogs in Washington State are likely to be part of the family vacation.[20]

If you want a lower investment, consider a freshwater fish. Buying the initial equipment to set up an aquarium can be up to $500 or more, but after that, you may spend around $100 per year to keep your fish friend fed and happy.[21]

Do not expect a bird to be an inexpensive pet. The cost of a bird is highly dependent on the type of bird you adopt. You can expect to spend from $250 to $1,000 annually. [22] These costs include food, maintaining their health, their environment and potential emergencies. And some species have very long lives. You must consider your African Grey parrot or your Amazon parrot as part of the family. With lifespans of thirty to fifty years or more, you should make provisions for them in case of your untimely demise.

Do you have formal or informal care directives for your pets? I know where my two cats will go if they outlive me. I know whose dog I might wind up adopting. And some people go as far as to make provisions for their pets in their wills or estates. If you want your bird to inherit your money, you must make a special provision and work with your attorney to make it legal.

If our pets die first, we mourn them. We might hold a funeral or a celebration of life. I am not just talking about a backyard burial (or the satin-lined soap box I used as a coffin when my pet mouse died when I was eight). Cremation is the most popular approach to dealing with your pet's remains. The cremation may be handled by a veterinarian or by a separate crematorium. But be careful when it comes to hanging on to those ashes—our life spans are typically much longer, so you could create quite a collection of urns. Other options include a traditional burial at home, or at a pet cemetery, taxidermy, or even mummification. If you opt to keep the ashes, you can have them made into memory stones, pottery, stained glass, or diamonds, or you can even launch them into space.[23]

While looking at statistics on pet funerals, I came across an industry performance report for pet cremation. One of the indicators listed as a driving factor was pet humanization.[24] That is precisely what we are exploring in this chapter. We have come to a place where we extend the same (or more) courtesy and inclusiveness to our pets than we do to other human beings. And if we consider those friends who write about being happy to share New Year's Eve with their dogs or cats or celebrate Mother's Day or Father's Day despite a lack of human children, we see the truth: we do think of our pets as family. The 2018 and 2022 *Pet Ownership and Demographics Sourcebooks* from the American Veterinary Medical Association supports this finding that 85 percent of dog owners and 76 percent of cat owners consider their pets family members.[25]

In 2020, a study conducted by Ameritrade found that 79 percent of pet owners called their pets their best friend, and that younger pet owners thought of their dog or cat as a starter child.[26] And in 2021, Americans collectively spent approximately $1.7 billion on Valentine's Day gifts for their pets.[27] I hope you all remember that chocolate is not healthy for your pets. But it can make people who write about your pets happy (hint, hint).

To understand how pets became such integral parts of our lives, we must delve into the societal shifts that have shaped our relationships with them over time.

How Did We Get Here?

How did our pets come to occupy such an elevated status in our lives? Sociologist Andrea Laurent-Simpson, author of *Just Like Family: How Companion Animals Joined the Household*, asserts that the multispecies family became prevalent after other societal and attitudinal shifts occurred. She sees the 1970s as when nontraditional family structures became more common—systems like single-parent families, children raised by grandparents, LGBTQ families, and childless-by-choice families. Our changed attitude toward animals can be traced back to the Industrial Revolution, when many families became more affluent and, therefore, able to focus on self-happiness and self-actualization. People with more time and money who moved away from agricultural work and into urban environments were inclined to interact with animals differently.[28]

During the height of COVID-19, more people adopted pets to keep them company during the lockdown. Over the years, the popularity of animals as pets and companions has grown, leading us to the present decade, the 2020s. In the United States, as of 2022, more households had pets than children: while 40 percent of households had children, 70 percent had pets. Our love of animals is a significant contributing factor to this statistic. But it is also due to an aging population, Boomers whose children have moved out, a decrease in the number of partners who opt to have children, and the fact that people are waiting longer to have children.[29]

These deep bonds that we feel with our animal companions come with benefits. For families who have opted to have only one child, or in single-parent families, pets can serve as important companions for children.

Research has shown that children with pets are likely to have more empathy toward others and increased self-esteem than their peers who do not have pets. And when a pet is viewed as a family member, sometimes the care of that pet takes on more meaning.[30] I can relate to this last item. I like a clean bathroom, and so do my cats. I do not enjoy scooping cat litter and cleaning out cat boxes. But I find myself thinking of it as "cleaning their bathroom."

We are most likely to reap the benefits from our relationship with our pets when we feel an attachment to them (later on, we'll delve into Buddhist perspectives on attachment and explore the potential risks of becoming overly attached to our pets). When our pets are friends or family, we become emotionally attached to them and those relationships. This is part of being human. And to derive the most benefit from these interspecies relationships, we need that emotional attachment. And we become more attached when we care for our pets and spend more time interacting with them. A study that considered people and their dogs shows that people care more and have stronger bonds with their house dogs than with dogs confined to the yard.[31]

Living with a pet can decrease your risk of heart disease, reduce stress, and lower your blood pressure. Having a pet as part of your life can help you maintain more emotional balance during difficult times. When other relationships are strained or while you are grieving, a pet can bring moments of relief.

Pets often become part of the community. "Dog people" become friends with other "dog people." Neighbors befriend each other's dogs and perhaps, through these relationships, one another. People socialize in dog parks or at the dog beach while their pups play. Sometimes families who do not have pets visit or help care for the pets of others. In this way, human-animal interactions expand. While I am a "cat person," I have more than one dog friend. There is one dog on the street whose house I pass when I walk. If I do not stop and pet and cuddle this dog, she will bark and whine for all to hear. Of course, I always make time to stop for her. And when I do, I often catch up with her human, who typically comes out when she hears the barking. It is not just dogs that create community. There are cat cafes, reptile houses, and other forums for bonding over your love of a specific breed or species.

> Consider the changes in society and family structures over the years. How have these shifts affected the way you view and treat your pets? Have you noticed a change in the role pets play in your life compared to previous generations? Does your attitude differ from that of your parents? What about your grandparents?

It's the emotional bond that truly solidifies the place of pets within our lives. This bond often transforms pets from mere companions to cherished members of our families.

As we explore the complex history that brought us here, it's important to consider the varying viewpoints on how we perceive our pets—whether they are beloved family members or unique companions in their own right.

Interspecies Family

Treating pets as family is a prevailing trend and will continue to grow and remain part of our culture for the foreseeable future. Not everyone embraces it, and its benefits are not universal. There are people with allergies, those who have had bad experiences, and those who do not agree that your fur baby deserves to be treated as anything more than an animal. This does not mean these are people who are abusive toward animals. It means they have a different perspective. They might not want to share a restaurant with an animal that is not a service animal, and they might not find it funny when your dog lifts his leg on the store mannequin. Where you see a friend or a family member, they see a dog.

You might cherish your dog or cat with the same depth of affection that others hold for their children. Think about a special pet you've had or currently have. How has this connection impacted your emotional well-being? In what ways has your pet provided companionship and support? Of course, you will grieve the loss of your beloved pet. But you expect to outlive your pet. You might even acquire another pet. A parent who loses a child has an entirely different experience. The fact that we extend our affection for people to our pets doesn't make our pets people.

Mark Wallace, a journalist and author, provides some perspective on what he sees as the truth behind our bond with our pets: "We love them because they aren't human, then spend their lives treating them like people. We don't want them to be animals wild, free, ultimately unknowable. We want them to be like us, but more static and predictable."

In his opinion piece, "Pets are Not People," Jeff Kunerth elaborates by stating, "The goal of being a parent is to raise your children to be independent, self-sufficient adults. We raise them to leave. The purpose of having a pet is to have something that remains attached to you, and you to them, until death." [32]

Some of my friends prefer to spend time at home with their animals and away from people. They feel that they derive enough companionship and affection from the animals sharing their homes. Yet they become angry when the dog digs up plants or chews on shoes. Or when one of the cats turns around and whacks them with claws out. We do not always want the digging, chewing, clawing version of our pet friends. We want the quiet, cuddly, good listener. And back to Wallace to drive this point home:

> We should remember that pets are extensions of us. We keep them to meet our needs, not theirs. Though we fantasize that person and pet meet as equals and join forces out of mutual admiration and respect, that's not how it is. Pets are biological Tamagotchi, and their dependence is absolute, built in to ensure their perpetual obedience. You can't "parent" a pet because you aren't teaching it how to leave you and become an independent being. Your pet is stuck with no choice but to love you. Even Snoopy, who lived wild and free in his mind, never left Charlie Brown. He knew who had the supper dish. [33]

Ouch. I like to think that my cats are happy living with me. That somewhere in their feline minds is relief that they have found their forever home. The truth just might be that in adopting them and keeping them from running away, I have simply created a codependent relationship, where the distribution of benefits is unequal.

Pets are not people, even if you call them your fur baby, roommate, grand-dog, or grand-cat. That does not mean that you cannot include them in your family or that you cannot have deep, meaningful relationships with them. Please remember the term *interspecies family.* You are not turning your pet into a person or human child. You are coming together and forming a bond that spans species. How do you navigate the balance between treating your pets as beloved companions while acknowledging their distinct needs and behaviors?

When you form a deep friendship with an animal, you are subject to the same type of attachment that you face with your human family and friends. As we move forward and take a closer look at Buddhist animal stories, teachings that feature animals, and guidelines for how to perceive animals, you will see that animals are to be respected, but you will not read about animals as family members. During the time of the Buddha, animals existed to serve a more practical purpose. That does not mean your inclusion of the cat in family pictures is some violation of Buddhist principles. It simply means that the interspecies family had not come into existence.

Animals have evolved on this planet with us. We first saw them as tools to assist us in our survival. As our lives became less treacherous, we began to view some of the animals around us as companions. We use them to tell stories, to provide entertainment and to teach life lessons. We lavish time, attention, and money on them. We turn to them for comfort. This is not going to change. While this was not how human-animal relationships worked during the time of the Buddha, you can still include the animals around you in your Buddhist practice. In this way you will:

- Live according to Buddhist morality as portrayed in the Jātaka tales.
- Create positive karma for both you and your pet.
- Strengthen your compassion practice.
- Understand how animals bring us cross-cultural connection.
- Draw on the life cycle of your pet to embrace impermanence.
- Sit with grief and other difficult emotions.
- Become a true guardian for your animal friends.

Let's look at some timeless teachings and include our animal companions so that they can act as guides on our spiritual path.

End Notes

[1] "The Evolution of Pet Ownership," PEDIGREE®, accessed September 26, 2023, https://www.pedigree.com/dog-care-articles/evolution-pet-ownership.
[2] "The Evolution of Pet Ownership."
[3] "The Evolution of Pet Ownership."
[4] "Silents Are Golden: Animal Stars of the Silent Era | Classic Movie Hub Blog," accessed August 6, 2023, https://www.classicmoviehub.com/blog/silents-are-golden-animal-stars-of-the-silent-era/.
[5] "Rin Tin Tin - Biography," IMDb, accessed August 6, 2023, https://www.imdb.com/name/nm0863833/bio/.
[6] "Rin Tin Tin - Biography."
[7] Lex Basu, "The 11 Best Animal TV Shows of All Time," AZ Animals, December 3, 2021, https://a-z-animals.com/blog/the-11-best-animal-tv-shows-of-all-time/.
[8] Basu.
[9] Stephen Messenger, "This Is The Very First Cat Video Posted To YouTube," The Dodo, November 1, 2014, https://www.thedodo.com/this-is-the-very-first-cat-vid-792883536.html.
[10] Jacob Yothment, "How Much of the World's Data Is Cat Content?," Pure Storage Blog, July 8, 2023, https://blog.purestorage.com/perspectives/how-much-of-the-worlds-data-is-cat-content/.
[11] Yothment.
[12] 11/12/2023 9:59:00 PM
[13] DigitalHubUSA, "Average Pet Parent Takes This Many Pictures of Their Pets Every Year," *Digitalhub US* (blog), August 26, 2022, https://swnsdigital.com/us/2022/08/average-pet-parent-takes-this-many-pictures-of-their-pets-every-year/.
[14] DigitalHubUSA, "Average Pet Parent Takes This Many Pictures of Their Pets Every Year," *Digitalhub US* (blog), August 26, 2022, https://swnsdigital.com/us/2022/08/average-pet-parent-takes-this-many-pictures-of-their-pets-every-year/.
[15] "People Who Love Animals More Than People: Psychology Of Empathy | BetterHelp," accessed August 6, 2023, https://www.betterhelp.com.
[16] "Pet Ownership Statistics and Facts in 2023 – Forbes Advisor," accessed August 6, 2023, https://www.forbes.com/advisor/pet-insurance/pet-ownership-statistics/.
[17] Elizabeth Gray, "Top 20 Pet Spending Statistics To Know In 2023: How Much Do We Spend On Pets?," Pet Keen, February 21, 2022, https://petkeen.com/pet-spending-statistics/.

[18] "Pet Ownership Statistics and Facts in 2023 – Forbes Advisor."
[19] "States With The Most Spoiled Dogs 2023 – Forbes Advisor," accessed August 6, 2023, https://www.forbes.com/advisor/pet-insurance/states-with-most-spoiled-dogs/.
[20] "States With The Most Spoiled Dogs 2023 – Forbes Advisor."
[21] Tom Kraeutler, "How Much Does It Really Cost to Keep Freshwater Fish?," *The Money Pit* (blog), December 15, 2018, https://www.moneypit.com/how-much-does-it-really-cost-to-keep-freshwater-fish/.
[22] Brooke Billingsley, "How Much Does a Pet Bird Cost? 2023 Price Guide," Pet Keen, February 4, 2021, https://petkeen.com/bird-cost/.
[23] Anthony Martin, "How Americans Are Buried Their Pets In (2021 Survey)," Choice Mutual, March 22, 2021, https://choicemutual.com/blog/pet-burials-2021/.
[24] "IBISWorld - Industry Market Research, Reports, and Statistics," accessed August 6, 2023, https://www.ibisworld.com/default.aspx.
[25] "States With The Most Spoiled Dogs 2023 – Forbes Advisor."
[26] Martin, "How Americans Are Buried Their Pets In (2021 Survey)."
[27] Gray, "Top 20 Pet Spending Statistics To Know In 2023."
[28] Southern Methodist University, "Sociologist Confirms What Pet Parents Know: Pets Really Are Part of the Family," accessed August 6, 2023, https://phys.org/news/2021-07-sociologist-pet-parents-pets-family.html.
[29] "A Stunning Stat: There Are More American Households With Pets Than Children," www.nar.realtor, March 13, 2023, https://www.nar.realtor/blogs/economists-outlook/a-stunning-stat-there-are-more-american-households-with-pets-than-children.
[30] L. F. Carver, "When Pets Are Family, the Benefits Extend into Society," The Conversation, January 6, 2019, http://theconversation.com/when-pets-are-family-the-benefits-extend-into-society-109179.
[31] Carver.
[32] "Pets Are Not People | University of Central Florida News," University of Central Florida News | UCF Today, August 19, 2020, https://www.ucf.edu/news/pets-are-not-people-even-if-we-pretend-they-are/.
[33] M. A. Wallace, "Sorry, But You're Not Your Dog's Mom," The Cut, October 27, 2016, https://www.thecut.com/2016/10/pets-are-not-children-so-stop-calling-them-that.html.

Chapter 2

Animals in Early Buddhism

In the Jātaka tales, we find a significant body of literature that tells the story of the Buddha before he was the Buddha. These are the stories of his many past lives. Jātaka means birth, and in these rebirths, he may have been a bird, a fish, a monkey, or a king. The Buddha was subject to karma and rebirth as he journeyed on his path as a *bodhisatta*. For our purposes, you might substitute the term Buddha-in-training *for bodhisatta*.

These stories are like parables or folklore. They can easily be misunderstood as children's stories, but they are not. The Jātaka can provide an entertaining introduction to Buddhism. Each story carries a deeper meaning and illustrates critical Buddhist teachings such as the Four Noble Truths and the Noble Eightfold Path. In these teachings we find the intersection of Buddhist concepts, with animals as wise and sentient beings. This sets the stage for our consideration of how we can have pets, befriend animals, and work toward enlightenment. Reviewing the Jātaka tales is an important first step toward developing an understanding of the role animals can play on our Buddhist path. To support that understanding, we need to learn more about the history of the Jātaka tales, the moral lessons they teach, and how animals help to portray the Buddha and some of his followers.

Introduction to the Jātaka Tales

Theravāda Buddhists rely on a series of texts called the Pāli canon. This large collection of early Buddhist teachings is considered to be the most complete collection of teachings directly attributed to the Buddha. The Buddha taught orally. His monks and nuns memorized and repeated his teachings. After the Buddha died, a meeting of his assembly of monks, or council, was called, and 500 *arhants* (enlightened monks) attended. The purpose of the meeting was to agree upon the correct version of the Buddha's teachings. His cousin, Ānanda, recited all of his teaching from memory. Ānanda, who was known for his excellent memory, had been the Buddha's attendant and was with him while he delivered many of his lessons. Another monk, Upāli, was in charge of reciting the rules of discipline or the *Vinaya*.

Scholars have varying opinions regarding when this council occurred, if it occurred, and what really happened. One version of the story has the meeting occurring three months after the Buddha's death. If that is true, then it makes sense that Ānanda and Upāli completed the recitations. Another version has this assembly not occurring until almost eighty years later. This makes it less likely that either of them participated. We are talking about a time frame of approximately between 483 and 400 BCE. The important takeaway is that the many teachings of the Buddha and the required discipline for monks was, at some point, agreed upon, memorized, and carried forward. In approximately the first century BCE, in Sri Lanka, this oral tradition was recorded in writing in the language of Pāli.

You may be wondering what any of this has to do with your pets and your spiritual practice. I promise I am getting there. Stick with me. My goal is to provide some overall context to the stories that we will use to consider the relationship between animals and the Buddha.

The Pāli canon is also referred to as the *Tipiṭaka,* which means triple baskets. The three baskets are the *suttas,* the *Vinaya,* and the *Abhidhamma*. The *Abhidhamma,* as we are discussing it here, is directly related to the teachings as initially captured and is a collection of summaries and expositions. This is an important distinction because later versions of the *Abhidhamma* from other Buddhist traditions are quite different.

The Jātaka tales fit within the *sutta* section of the three baskets. The *suttas* are grouped into five *nikāyas,* or collections. One of these collections is called the *Khuddaka Nikaya,* the division of short books. And one of these short books is the Jātakas. Although with 547 stories, it might not seem like a short book. Each of the stories is short, and most follow a similar format. The first section is a "story of the present" this explains when, where, and, most importantly, why the Buddha tells the past-life story. Then comes the actual past-life birth story. Then at the end of the story, the Buddha reveals who the various people in the past life are now.

Excerpts from the *Kharādiya-Jātaka* demonstrate this well-used method of storytelling.

Part I, the story of the present:

> This story was told by the Master while at Jetavana about an unruly Brother. Tradition says that this Brother was unruly and would not heed admonition. Accordingly, the Master asked him, saying, "Is it true, as they say, that you are unruly and will not heed admonition?"
>
> "It is true, Blessed One," was the reply.
>
> "So too in bygone days," said the Master, "you were unruly and would not heed the admonition of the wise and good, with the result that you were caught in a gin and met your death." And so, saying, he told this story of the past.

Part II, the past-life birth story:

> Once on a time when Brahmadatta was in Benares the Bodhisatta was born a deer and dwelt in the forest at the head of a herd of deer. His sister brought her son to him, saying, "Brother, this is your nephew; teach him deer's ruses." And thus, she placed her son under the Bodhisatta's care. Said the latter to his nephew, "Come at such and such a time and I will give you a lesson." But the nephew made no appearance at the time appointed. And, as on that day, so on seven days did he skip his lesson and fail to learn the ruses of deer; and at last, as he was roaming about, he was caught in a gin. His mother came and said to the Bodhisatta, "Brother, was not your nephew taught deer's ruses?"
>
> "Take no thought for the unteachable rascal," said the Bodhisatta; [160] "your son failed to learn the ruses of deer." And so, saying, having lost all desire to advise the scapegrace even in his deadly

peril, he repeated this stanza:

For when a deer has twice four hoofs to run
And branching antlers armed with countless tines,
And when by seven tricks he's saved himself,
I teach him then, Kharādiyā, no more.
But the hunter killed the self-willed deer that was caught in the snare and departed with its flesh.

Part III, the identification of the main characters:

When the Master had ended this lesson in support of what he had said as to the unruliness of the Brother in bygone days as well as in the present, he shewed the connection, and identified the Birth, by saying "In those days this unruly Brother was the nephew-deer, Uppala-vaṇṇā was the sister, and I myself the deer who gave the admonition." [1]

The Jātakas were developed during the fourth century BCE. It is challenging to locate a precise date as there are many stories, and they originate from different regions. Some tales probably come from before the birth of the Buddha, and some were created later. Although they are part of the Pāli canon, they are not unique to Buddhism. These tales serve as valuable insight into the history of the society and the political, social, and religious structures of that time. [2] These are not stories that are unique to Buddhism; they are stories that were part of the cultural identity while followers of the Buddha were developing relatable ways of teaching Buddhist ideas.

Animals in the Jātaka Tales

The most famous Jātaka tale is the story of the starving tigress. It is very possible that you have heard or read this story. It is used to illustrate the lengths to which the Bodhisatta would go to show compassion to another sentient being. The Bodhisatta and a companion came across a starving tigress. She was weak and emaciated. She also had babies. The Bodhisatta could see that the tigress was become crazed from hunger and was beginning to see her cubs as food. He sent his companion off to look for food. But the tigress began to act as if she were about to eat her babies. Seeing this, the Bodhisatta thought of the tragedy that would occur if she were to eat her own offspring. Of the suffering she would endure when she realized what she had done. Of the confusion and the suffering of the whelps as their own mother attacked them. And so, the Bodhisatta flung himself off a cliff and landed, dead, in the bushes. The tigress investigated, ate his flesh, and regained her strengthen. She did not kill her cubs; she was able to nurse them, and they survived.[3]

The purpose of this story is to impress upon others the great compassion possessed by the Buddha in his past and current life, as he was willing to give up his own life to feed another sentient being and to prevent her from an action that would bring about suffering and bad karma. This Jātaka does not appear in the Pāli canon. It is generally accepted as a later addition. This story helps to emphasize the definition of a *bodhisatta* as a compassionate being, or one who continues to return after reaching enlightenment in order to help beings reach that same goal. If we were to categorize the versions of the Jātaka tales as belonging to different schools of Buddhism, you might place the story of the starving tigress with

Mahāyāna (Chinese) and also with Vajrayana (Tibetan) Buddhism. This is not to imply that Theravāda Buddhism is not concerned with compassionate behavior. Each group embraces the importance of the Jātakas in their way. And the role of the *bodhisatta* has a different emphasis. Similarly, we are looking at these stories with an eye for how animals feature, and how that informs our relationships with our pets and sets the tone for our Buddhist practice.

In the Jātaka tales, the Buddha is shown living as various animals, including a hare, woodpecker, deer, monkey king, elephant, buffalo, and many others.[4] A preliminary count indicates that monkeys appear most frequently in these tales (around twenty-seven times), followed by elephants (twenty-four appearances), jackals (twenty times), and lions (nineteen appearances). Crows are the most prominent birds, appearing in at least seventeen stories. As a general guideline, monkeys may depict a lack of wisdom, and elephants are complex and intelligent, while jackals and crocodiles can be untrustworthy.[5] However, these guidelines do not always hold true. As you will see from some of the stories cited here, there are instances where a monkey teaches leadership to a king and an elephant is cruel.

If an animal in one of the stories exhibits desirable behavior, that animal was either the Buddha in a past life or one of his close and well-regarded monks or followers. Devadatta, who was intensely jealous of the Buddha and tried (and failed) to have him killed shows up, too: predictably, he usually engages in unethical, cruel, and dishonest actions.

The majority of stories depicting animals portray them in their natural habitats rather than as pets or companions. At the time of the Buddha, only kings had the wealth and means to keep animals that others used for labor or food. Keeping an elephant required space, large amounts of food, and a challenging taming process. Yet for a king, an elephant was a sign of prosperity and power—and a necessity for rituals and wars. There is a parallel there to today's world in that wealthy nations have the ability to spend the most money on pet ownership.

In one story, a king handed a wild elephant over to his trainer. The trainer poked the elephant with a sharp stick, beat the elephant, and used cruel methods to tame the elephant. In pain and in fear for his life, the elephant broke away from the trainer. While the elephant was never caught, he also lived in constant fear of being recaptured and beaten. Even a light breeze would startle him. At that time, the Bodhisatta was a tree sprite (in Buddhist *suttas* there is an acknowledgement of tree spirits and other entities). The tree sprite observed the fearful elephant and said:

> Fear'st thou the wind that ceaselessly
> The rotten boughs doth rend always?
> Such fear will waste thee quite away! [6]

These words calmed the elephant, and his fears subsided.

In this story, the elephant represented a follower of the Buddha who lived in fear of death. He was afraid of everything and everyone. In the follower's current life, the Buddha taught him the Four Noble Truths, and the man took on the Noble Eightfold Path and lost his fear. [7]

In the Jātakas, some of the animals are highly anthropomorphized; they speak and act much like humans do. Very often these animals represent the past lives of other humans. Dr. Reiko Ohnuma, author of *Unfortunate Destiny: Animals in the Indian Buddhist Imagination*, calls these portrayals foreshadowing of humans. She posits that they receive special treatment because they are meant to remind us that these are animals who later become humans. However, she also provides another perspective: these stories are a version of folk tales, many of which are not Buddhist in origin. They come from the local tradition and were adopted into Buddhist literature. In the folk tales, the animals are allegorical humans. As you read some of the samples provided, you can see both angles: the past lives of key Buddhist figures before they were human and animal characters used to entertain and teach life lessons.[8]

Within the Buddhist system of rebirth, there are more than thirty planes of existence and six realms. This means there are more than thirty scenarios where a being can be reborn, and those scenarios exist under six different categories. The animal realm is one of the three lower realms, along with the land of hungry ghosts and the hell realm. It is better to be an animal than to be a hungry ghost or a hell creature. As a human, you are in the best possible situation because you have access to Buddhist teachings and the ability to end the cycle of suffering. You do not have to believe in rebirth to see that most humans have better lives than most animals. While you give your pet a secure and happy life, many animals live in a constant state of hunting or being hunted, searching for safe shelter from the elements and from the dangers of the wild or urban world.

Even though I think my cats have it made and we utter the phrase "It's a dog's life," this is not the goal, and they are not in the best rebirth. Once born or reborn as an animal, it is extremely difficult to make it out of this realm. In the *Bālapṇḍitasutta* (MN 129), the Buddha says, "I could tell you many different things about the animal realm. So much so that it's not easy to completely describe the suffering in the animal realm."

In these tales where animals may show wisdom or behave ethically, it is not because this behavior is widespread within the animal realm; it is because within the context of the stories of the Buddha in his past lives, the inclusion of animals is a skillful teaching device.

Every Jātaka tale exists to showcase a clear example of how to live and how to follow the Noble Eightfold path. The combined anthology shows how much effort it takes to reach a lifetime where it is possible to obtain nirvana. Taken as a whole, we see the challenges we face in overcoming our own suffering. We also learn that it is possible. The point is not that the Buddha is the only one who achieved liberation; it is that he is one who did, and now we have his example.

Let's consider some of the animal-centric stories and how they can help us.

Animal Jātakas and Their Themes

Support and Generosity

Less dramatic than the story of the starving tigress but with a similar outcome is the Sasa-Jātaka. In this story, the Bodhisatta is a rabbit. A brahmin (a religious man) is on alms round and asks the rabbit for food.

Even today, in some countries (such as Thailand), Buddhist monks go out with bowls, and the local community gives them food. There is a purposefully interdependent relationship between the monks and the laypeople. Today, monks do not ask rabbits or any animal other than humans for food. But in this Jātaka tale, the brahmin asked four animals for alms: an otter, a monkey, a jackal, and a rabbit. Each animal responded by sharing the spoils from their own hunt or foraging. The otter had fish to give. The monkey contributed some fruit, and the jackal provided lizard meat and milk curds. The rabbit only ate grass and realized that grass was unsuitable for a human, so when it was his turn, he offered himself up as a meal. This passage describes what happened next:

> Rising from his bed of kuça grass and coming to the place, he thrice shook himself that if there were any insects within his coat, they might escape death. Then offering his whole body as a free gift he sprang up, and like a royal swan, alighting on a cluster of lotuses, in an ecstasy of joy he fell on the heap of live coals. But the flame failed even to heat the pores of the hair on the body of the Bodhisatta, and it was as if he had entered a region of frost. Then he addressed Sakka in these words: "Brahmin, the fire you have kindled is icy-cold: it fails to beat even the pores of the hair on my body. What is the meaning of this?"
>
> "Wise sir," he replied, "I am no brahmin. I am Sakka, and I have come to put your virtue to the test." The Bodhisatta said, "If not only thou, Sakka, but all the inhabitants of the world were to try me in this matter of almsgiving, they would not find in me any unwillingness to give," and with this the Bodhisatta uttered a cry of exultation like a lion roaring.

Then said Sakka to the Bodhisatta, "O wise hare, be thy virtue known throughout a whole eon." And squeezing the mountain, with the essence thus extracted, he daubed the sign of a hare on the orb of the moon. And after depositing the hare on a bed of young kuça grass, in the same wooded part of the jungle, Sakka returned to his own place in heaven.[9]

Sakka was the King of the Gods. In this story, the Buddha identified the animals as some of his most devoted followers and senior monks: the otter was Ānanda, while the jackal was Moggallāna, and the monkey as Sāriputta. [10]

In the *Sasa-Jātaka,* we see this big theme of the rabbit willingly giving his life to feed a holy man. And we understand that this was really a test. We also learn that it is the role of non-monks (in this story, the animals) to support the efforts of monks (the brahmin). The rabbit did not have to die; he just had to show how far he was willing to go to support the brahmin. A holy man deserves your maximum support. If you compare the gifts that each animal was preparing to give, you see that while the otter, jackal, and monkey were all generous, it was the rabbit, the past life of the Buddha, who was willing to give everything.

Together, the otter, jackal, monkey, and rabbit show us the importance of our spiritual community, and specifically, they teach us to provide support to our Buddhist teachers. We also see that one who is further along on the path has no qualms about giving everything. This tale is about what a willingness to give does for you, not about others actually gaining from your gift.

As we grapple with the truth of suffering, we see that attachment comes from greed. It is not wrong to enjoy life and to enjoy the people around you. Our suffering comes from not being satisfied, from wanting the good times to never end. The cure for greed is generosity. In what way can you direct generosity toward your pet or toward other animals? As you spend time with your animal friends, do you feel called to help them with food or shelter or to give them reassurance? If you are a person who feels challenged by other people, you can direct your generosity to your furry, feathered, or scaly friends.

Generosity and Compassion, Not Foolishness

Once there was a woodpecker who saw a lion with a bone wedged in his throat. The lion could not eat and was going to starve to death. Now, if you are a woodpecker, flying close to a lion is a very bad idea. Yet this woodpecker saw the lion suffering and knew that he could help him. But would he lose his life in the process of helping the lion? This is the dilemma presented to us in the *Javasakuṇa-Jātaka*. The woodpecker quickly advised the lion that he could save his life, and in turn the lion must not take his life. Feeling cautiously optimistic, the woodpecker took a stick and used it to wedge the lion's jaws open. He then hopped into the lion's mouth, pulled the bone out of his throat, kicked away the stick, and quickly flew to safety. The lion made a full recovery.

At a later time, the woodpecker came across that same lion. He reminded the lion that he saved his life and asked the lion for a favor. The lion said to the woodpecker:

> To trust thy head to a lion's jaw.
> A creature red in tooth and claw,
> To dare such a deed and be living still,
> Is token enough of my good will.

The woodpecker realized that if he was within reach, this time the lion would eat him. So he flew away. In this story, the Buddha was the woodpecker, and Devadatta was the lion.[11] From this story, we learn that the Buddha extended compassion to those who would do him harm. We learn not to assume that helping others will change their true nature.

This lesson also offers up a reminder: do not expect wild animals to be anything other than what they are. We should still do the best we can to help them and to offer them compassion and make their lives easier, but we should never expect a lion to be anything other than a lion. This is the lesson for us as we seek to help us balance our relationships with animals and our Buddhist practice.

Let Go of Self

In a past life, the Buddha was the king of the monkeys. His monkeys enjoyed the fruit of an enormous mango tree. The king of the humans found about this tree and wanted the fruit for his people. The king sent his troops to claim the tree. They surrounded the tree, with the goal of killing the monkeys for their meat and taking the fruit. The monkeys were trapped and faced certain death. The monkey king saw an escape route. He would stretch out from the tree and grab a nearby bamboo shoot, and the monkeys could use him as a bridge to escape.

In this past-life story, Devadatta was an envious monkey who sought to harm the monkey king. As Devadatta ran away, he climbed up high and jumped onto the back of the monkey king, hitting him so hard that he broke the body of the monkey king.

Seeing the monkey king sacrifice himself for his subjects caused the human king to understand that it was wrong to harm the monkey king and the other monkeys. He stopped the attack and had the monkey king brought to him so that he could have a comfortable and peaceful death. Before he died, the monkey king told the human king that he knew it was his role to guard his subjects and that he had no fear of death since he knew his monkeys escaped to freedom. He also advised the human king that a leader places the welfare of his subjects first.

And after imparting this leadership lesson to the human king, the monkey died and received the recognition and ceremony of human royalty. In this story, called the *Mahākapi-Jātaka*, the human king was Ānanda, and the other monkeys were the followers of the Buddha.[12]

Once again, the Buddha sacrifices himself in order to help others. In this case, he gives all for his followers. That is a theme that echoes across religions and philosophy. You might think of the Christian teachings of Jesus as the messiah. Or perhaps the idea of the good of the many outweighing the good of the few. We can think about this as an ability to let go of self. The Buddha as monkey king had no attachment to his body or to his perception of self. He was free from ego. Devadatta reminded us that when you act out of kindness and compassion, someone might take advantage, but you should do the right thing anyway.

Contemplating this story and how it might be applicable to our theme of our pets and our practice, I remembered the first time I interacted with a small local animal rescue. I was shocked at how rudely I was treated. The person who spoke with me seemed annoyed that I was interrupting his day. He was also angry with me that I did not know that if a feral cat had a clipped ear, it meant that cat had already been trapped, neutered, and returned to the wild. I left feeling hurt and embarrassed. I was never going to bother with that group again. But later, after I let my feelings work through me, my attitude and opinion shifted. Sometimes, people can be the most comfortable with animals. Perhaps other humans have caused them physical and physiological harm.

> Was I going to let my ego get in the way of supporting a group that was helping hundreds of lost, hurt, and hungry animals? What would you do in a similar situation?

What Is the Message?

These stories teach us how the Bodhisatta became the Buddha. They include strong, resounding messages to be compassionate, be generous even to those who seem undeserving, and be willing to let go of your ego. Next, let's consider some other qualities that we need to foster in order to step closer to enlightenment, as taught to us by our animal friends in the Jātakas.

Be Modest

In his current life, a wealthy man had a bit of a meltdown in public and removed all his clothing. In the *Nacca-Jātaka*, we learn that in a past life, that man was a peacock who became so excited when the Mallard Princess chose him to be her husband, that he threw open his wings and exposed himself to the crowd. This passage makes me think of a flasher in a trench coat. The princess's father, the Golden Mallard King, immediately found the peacock to be unworthy and selected another husband for his daughter. [13]

Avoid Greed

A crow and a pigeon took up residency in the kitchen of a wealthy man. Each day they left to find food. Seeing all the wonderful food in the kitchen, the crow decided not to forage for his own food. The pigeon warned the crow, but the crow was greedy and wanted the food that was being prepared for the humans. The cooks caught the crow stealing a piece of fish and captured the crow, who then became part of the evening meal. In this story (the *Kapota-Jātaka*), because he was a friend of the crow, the pigeon was sent away. [14]

Be Fair and Impartial

The *Kukkura-Jātaka* reminds us that bias and discrimination have existed for thousands of years. The king discovered that some dogs had chewed the leather straps on the royal carriage. In retaliation, he ordered the death of all stray dogs. Purebred palace dogs were safe. Before the killing began, a stray dog snuck into the king's chambers and provided proof that it was the palace dogs who did the chewing. The king was horrified by his own thoughts and behavior. He had perceived the wild dogs as lesser in status and assumed they were poorly behaved. From that point forward, the king supplied all dogs with good food, and he spent the rest of his days protecting animals and engaging in charitable acts. [15]

Resist Overconfidence

In the *Cammasāṭaka-Jātaka,* a ram killed a monk in two separate lifetimes. In both instances, a merchant warned the monk that the ram was going to attack. Both times the monk assumed that the ram was stepping back in order to show him respect. Both times, the monk was wrong. The ram was actually gathering speed and strength so that he could run right over the monk. Fool me once, shame on you. Fool me twice, shame on me. [16]

Be Loyal to Your Partner

In the *Kakkaṭā-Jātaka,* a woman and her husband were elephants in a past life. They and the other members of their herd lived near a lake. This could have been idyllic, except for one giant problem: a crab so large that he could easily capture and eat elephants. Any elephant who went to the lake ran the risk of becoming crab food.

The husband elephant was brave. He decided that he would defeat this crab and bring peace back to the herd. He encouraged the other elephants to go to the lake and drink their fill. He would be the last one in the line to leave, and that would make him the first elephant that the crab would attack. All went well until the crab grabbed the brave elephant, and the brave elephant was unable to break free. The entire herd ran away. Only the wife stayed nearby. Using her most charming voice and lots of flattery, she convinced the crab to let her husband go. Then when the crab released her husband, he turned around and crushed the crab.[17]

Draw upon Truth, Foresight, Fixed Resolve, and Fearlessness

Sometimes people think that being a Buddhist is all peaceful meditation and no conflict. I have listened to spirited debate around whether Buddhists are even allowed to defend themselves. I do seek to avoid harming others, but there is nothing in my Buddhism that encourages me to be a doormat. We are going to have conflict. We will encounter others who may wish to do us harm, and our goal is to use right view, right intention, and right actions to skillfully find a way to resolve the conflict.

In the *Vānarinda-Jātaka*, the Bodhisatta was a monkey who outwitted a crocodile by understanding the behavior of the crocodile, keeping his cool, and using his intellect to jump away with his life.

A crocodile's wife was pregnant and craving monkey meat. Her husband knew of the perfect monkey to catch. This monkey was big and strong. Each day this monkey crossed the river by leaping from rock to rock to reach an island that had plenty of mangoes and breadfruit. The crocodile decided to pose as a rock. When the monkey jumped on him, he would open his jaws and capture the monkey. But the monkey noticed that one of the rocks in the river looked a bit off. It was higher out of the water than usual. He did not remember seeing this rock during his other crossings.

The monkey called out to the rock three times. And on that third attempt, the crocodile fell for it: he answered and admitted that he was no rock. The crocodile assumed that the monkey was trapped and would eventually have to jump in his direction. The clever monkey told the crocodile that he knew he was defeated. He told the crocodile to open his mouth and that he would jump in.

This is not a story of self-sacrifice. This story is about being aware, being clever, and having your wits about you. When a crocodile opens its mouth, it shuts its eyes. So as the crocodile waited with an open mouth and closed eyes, the monkey landed on his head, and before the crocodile realized what had happened, the monkey was gone. The story ends with the crocodile exclaiming:

> Monkey, he that in this world possesses the four virtues
> overcomes his foes. And you, methinks, possess all four." And,
> so saying, he repeated this stanza:
>
> Whose, O monkey-king, like you, combines
> Truth, foresight, fixed resolve, and fearlessness,
> Shall see his routed foemen turn and flee. [18]

The Message

What we have just read is a sample—we did not cover all of the Jātaka tales or even all of the Jātaka tales with animals. And the point of the stories is not that elephants are brave, and monkeys can be wise, and that crows are greedy, and crabs are dangerous. The use of animals helps to take away some of our bias toward other humans and simply reveals admirable ways of being. The lesson is how to be a good human, and animals highlight the behaviors that can be attributed to those who follow the Noble Eightfold Path.

> What do you make of all of this? In what way will these stories become part of your practice? Have you ever considered that as you live a more ethical life you will become a better advocate for animals and a better friend to your pet?

The Importance of the Jātaka Tales

While many of the Jātaka tales are borrowed from the popular stories of the time, when the Buddha sat under the Bodhi tree meditating, he attained three forms of knowledge. The first being the ability to discern all of his previous lives. This passage from the *Majjhima Nikāya* tells us how this came to pass:

> When the mind was thus concentrated, purified, bright, unblemished, rid of defilement, pliant, malleable, steady, and attained to imperturbability, I directed it to the knowledge of recollecting my past lives. I recollected my manifold past lives, i.e., one birth, two…five, ten…fifty, a hundred, a thousand, a hundred thousand, many eons of cosmic contraction, many eons of cosmic expansion, many eons of cosmic contraction and expansion: "There I had such a name, belonged to such a clan, had such an appearance. Such was my food, such my experience of pleasure and pain, such the end of my life. Passing away from that state, I re-arose there. There too I had such a name, belonged to such a clan, had such an appearance. Such was my food, such my experience of pleasure and pain, such the end of my life. Passing away from that state, I re-arose here." Thus, I remembered my manifold past lives in their modes and details.

This was the first knowledge I attained in the first watch of the night. (MN 36)

You do not have to accept rebirth to benefit from these stories. Each one has a self-contained lesson, and all contain a reminder that the journey to enlightenment is long and arduous but achievable. In many of the Jātakas, the Buddha begins by saying, "When I was just an unenlightened Bodhisatta…" This shows that there is hope for those of us who are unenlightened. [19]

Beyond the intended teaching of each story, we have an opportunity to extend those messages to our daily interactions with our pets and our relationships with the animal world around us. Have any of these stories inspired you to look at your human-animal relationships differently? Are there scenarios where you might become an even greater advocate for animal welfare?

Some animals receive consistent treatment, like the deceitful crocodile pretending to be a rock. Most of the time, when an animal is wise or compassionate or has desirable traits, that animal is revealed as the Bodhisatta himself or a past-life version of one of his more senior monks.

In some stories, the same species of animal plays the role of both good and evil. Remember that in the *Mahākapi-Jātaka,* the Bodhisatta was the self-sacrificing monkey king, and Devadatta was also a monkey, albeit an evil one. And in the *Laṭukika-Jātaka*, the Bodhisatta is a kindly leader of the elephants who protects a quail's nest as his herd marches past. He warns the mother quail that coming behind the herd is a rogue elephant who will not follow his lead. He urges the quail to ask the rogue elephant to show her the same courtesy and avoid trampling on her nest. In response to her request, the rogue elephant says:

> I will slay thy young ones, quail;
> What can thy poor help avail?
> My left foot can crush with ease
> Many thousand birds like these.[20]

You guessed it. Devadatta was that rogue elephant.

To read a story where there is a good monkey and an evil monkey or a compassionate elephant and an unkind elephant is an excellent reminder that we are not completely bad, nor are we completely good. We are finding our way on the path, and we experience the results of our decisions and our actions. Or as the *Upajjhatthana Sutta* reminds us, "I am the owner of my actions, heir to my actions, born of my actions, related through my actions, and have my actions as my arbitrator. Whatever I do, for good or for evil, to that will I fall heir." (AN 5.57)

How Is this Relevant Today?

These stories show the Buddha living in the world and seeking to solve the problems that humans face. Like so many of the Buddha's teachings, these stories are easy to read and comprehend. There is wisdom there for all of us: a reminder to follow the Noble Eightfold Path.

Animals are their own unique beings. They are worthy of our respect and compassion. Animals have emotions. Sometimes they outwit humans or help other animals. When they speak, they use language to communicate about being an animal. They are most often truthful. [21]

In visiting the Jātaka tales and sharing them with you, it occurs to me that I have my own tale. It's the story of the cat, the mockingbird, and the college student. During my final year of college, I rented a room in a house, providing me with a peaceful environment to complete my degree without the typical roommate drama.

One day, as I was walking from my car to the front door, I felt a whoosh of air. Out of the corner of my eye, I saw a mockingbird flying away. I was surprised at how low the bird was flying and how close it must have come to my head. The next day, on my way to the front door, a mockingbird swooped down from the roof, and I felt like it was going to dive bomb right into my head. I ducked and ran into the house. For almost a week, the mockingbird came at me every time I came up the walkway. I asked my landlady if she was having the same experience. She laughed and implied that I was imaging these attacks.

One day, the next-door neighbor observed me running from the mockingbird. The neighbor called out to me, and from the safety of the front porch, I spoke with her. She told me that she had seen my cat stalking a bird, presumably the one that was stalking me. And together, we surmised that somehow the bird associated me with the cat and considered me to be a threat.

In this story, none of the animals talk. I do not know for certain if my cat was harassing the bird and if, in turn, the bird decided to harass me. As far as I know, no creature in this story is a future Buddha. But I do know that each of us, the bird, the cat, and I, was trying to coexist in an urban environment, each of us looking for a safe and peaceful home. None of us wanted to feel threatened or under attack.

Each day that you share your life with an animal is an opportunity for you to be part of your own Jātaka tale. Maybe you do not interact with crocodiles and monkeys and elephants (although maybe you do), but each day with your pet you are seeking more happiness and freedom from suffering. Your dog, cat, fish, reptile, or ferret is on this journey with you.

All Are Subject to Karma

For thousands of years, humans have hunted animals for food. It is only natural that tales of hunters and the hunted appear in Buddhist literature. In the *Kuruṅga-Jātaka,* we find a hunter stalking antelope. Instead of tracking and chasing the antelope, the hunter built a clever trap. He built himself a platform in a fruit tree and threw some of the fruit to the ground as bait. Then he settled in and waited for an antelope to eat the fruit. An antelope spied the fruit but somehow had a sense that something was wrong. Out of frustration, the hunter threw more fruit to the ground. Rather than bring the antelope within range, the antelope ran away. The angry hunter yelled at the fleeing antelope:

> "Begone! I've missed you this time." Wheeling round, the Bodhisatta halted and said, "You may have missed me, my good man; but depend upon it, you have not missed the reward of your conduct, namely, the eight Large and the sixteen Lesser hells and all the five forms of bonds and torture." With these words the

antelope bounded off on its way; and the hunter, too, climbed down and went his way.²²

In this story, the antelope was the Buddha in a past life, and the hunter was Devadatta. Here is the continued lesson of how for many lifetimes, Devadatta tried unsuccessfully to harm the Buddha. The core teaching is that of karma. Our actions and intentions are not without result. Devadatta's desire to kill the Buddha and the fact that he acted on that desire has generated so much negative karma that Devadatta will experience rebirth in multiple hell realms. The eight Large hells consist of constant torture in many forms. Each one has a primary torture. For example, in the first, or Saṁjīva, beings are constantly tortured and kept awake via strong winds. In the second, or Kālasūtra, beings are sliced apart over and over again with a black string. The sixteen Lesser hells represent compartments within the Large hells, each one with its own specific forms of torture. Examples of these punishments include starvation, thirst, or fire. ²³

We see that our actions shape our karma and our karma shapes our experiences and our future rebirths. We do not see a condemnation against hunting. Devadatta is not in danger because he was a hunter; he will suffer because he wished to harm the Buddha. This story was told within the context of a time when people hunted for their food. We will discuss the challenges around Buddhist teachings and our treatment of animals in a future chapter.

Right now, just remember that all beings are subject to karma and the cycle of rebirth. This means all animals, pets or otherwise. The challenges of karma and rebirth and our animal friends is where we next turn our attention.

End Notes

[1] "Sacred Texts: Buddhism," accessed December 3, 2015, http://www.sacred-texts.com/bud/index.htm#jataka.

[2] "Jatakas as Valuable Source Of Information On Ancient India - GKToday," accessed September 27, 2023, https://www.gktoday.in/jatakas-as-valuable-source-of-information-on-ancient-india/.

[3] J. S. Speyer, "Jatakamala or Garland of Birth Stories – 1. The Story of the Tigress," accessed August 13, 2023, https://www.ancient-buddhist-texts.net/English-Texts/Garland-of-Birth-Stories/01-The-Story-of-the-Tigress.htm.

[4] "The Jataka Tales: Why They Remain Relevant for Adults and Children Both; All of the Buddhist Teachings Contained in Stories - Buddha Weekly: Buddhist Practices, Mindfulness, Meditation," April 28, 2018, https://buddhaweekly.com/the-jataka-tales-why-they-remain-relevant-for-adults-and-children-both-all-of-the-buddhist-teachings-contained-in-stories/.

[5] "JSTOR: History of Religions, Vol. 40, No. 1 (Aug., 2000), Pp. 58-81," accessed March 31, 2013, http://www.jstor.org/stable/3176513?&Search=yes&searchText=Gold&searchText=Purple&searchText=Robes&list=hide&searchUri=%2Faction%2FdoBasicSearch%3FQuery%3DRobes%2BPurple%2Band%2BGold%26acc%3Don%26wc%3Don%26fc%3Doff&prevSearch=&item=2&ttl=674&returnArticleService=showFullText.

[6] "The Jataka, Volume I: Book I.--Ekanipāta: No. 15. Kharādiya-Jātaka," accessed August 6, 2023, https://sacred-texts.com/bud/j1/j1018.htm.

[7] "The Jataka, Volume I: Book I.--Ekanipāta: No. 15. Kharādiya-Jātaka."

[8] "Talk by Reiko Ohnuma at Stanford University - YouTube," accessed August 6, 2023, https://www.youtube.com/watch?v=NRNNJACWZh4.

[9] "The Jataka, Vol. III: No. 316.: Sasa-Jātaka.," accessed August 6, 2023, https://sacred-texts.com/bud/j3/j3017.htm.

[10] "The Jataka, Vol. III: No. 316.: Sasa-Jātaka."

[11] "The Jataka, Vol. III: No. 308.: Javasakuṇa-Jātaka.," accessed October 2, 2023, https://sacred-texts.com/bud/j3/j3009.htm.

[12] "The Jataka, Vol. III: No. 407.: Mahākapi-Jātaka.," accessed August 6, 2023, https://sacred-texts.com/bud/j3/j3108.htm.

[13] "The Jataka, Volume I: Book I.--Ekanipāta: No. 32. Nacca-Jātaka," accessed August 6, 2023, https://sacred-texts.com/bud/j1/j1035.htm.

[14] "The Jataka, Volume I: Book I.--Ekanipāta: No. 42. Kapota-Jātaka," accessed August 6, 2023, https://sacred-texts.com/bud/j1/j1045.htm.

[15] "The Jataka, Volume I: Book I.--Ekanipāta: No. 22. Kukkura-Jātaka," accessed August 6, 2023, https://sacred-texts.com/bud/j1/j1025.htm.

[16] "The Jataka, Vol. III: No. 324.: Cammasāṭaka-Jātaka.," accessed August 13, 2023, https://sacred-texts.com/bud/j3/j3025.htm.

[17] "The Jataka, Vol. II: Book III. Tika-Nipāta: No. 267. Kakkatā-Jātaka," accessed August 6, 2023, https://sacred-texts.com/bud/j2/j2120.htm.

[18] "The Jataka, Volume I: Book I.--Ekanipāta: No. 57. Vānarinda-Jātaka," accessed August 6, 2023, https://sacred-texts.com/bud/j1/j1060.htm.

[19] "Talk by Reiko Ohnuma at Stanford University - YouTube.""The Jataka Tales."

[20] "The Jataka, Vol. III: No. 357.: Laṭukika-Jātaka.," accessed August 6, 2023, https://sacred-texts.com/bud/j3/j3058.htm.

[21] "Talk by Reiko Ohnuma at Stanford University - YouTube."

[22] "The Jataka, Volume I: Book I.--Ekanipāta: No. 21. Kuruṅga-Jātaka," accessed August 6, 2023, https://sacred-texts.com/bud/j1/j1024.htm.

[23] "Hells in Buddhism," Hells in Buddhism | Buddhism & Healing, December 17, 2017, https://buddhism.redzambala.com/buddhism/philosophy/hells-in-buddhism.html.

Chapter 3

Animal Rebirth

Looking out the kitchen window, I saw this big, fluffy, gray-and-white cat watching me. At first, I ignored her. She looked clean, healthy, and well-fed. I finished the dishes and walked away. An hour later, I returned to the kitchen, and there she was, looking in the window and meowing. I went outside to say hello. Maybe she would run from me, and that would be it. She did not run from me; she ran to me. When I bent over to pet her, she jumped into my arms. She was clearly seeking a human connection—or as we would later joke, a human host. This cat knew that the human-feline relationship was critical to her survival. She was not cut out to be a street cat. I named her Alex because initially I was uncertain of her gender, so I selected a name that could fit either Alexander or Alexis.

Alex was not an easy cat. She came into a household with two other cats who were living in harmony: Soho, who was the alpha, and Maple, who accepted her role as the follower. At first, things went well. Alex and Maple got along well and ran through the house playing. One day, when Alex and Maple were running around, I found that one of them had had an accident on our comforter. If this were a drama, that spot of cat urine would have been the foreshadowing of danger to come.

Things quickly escalated. Soho, who was as mellow as they come, a benevolent alpha (or so we thought), attacked Alex. One moment, Soho was sitting across the room staring at Alex, and the next he ran full speed at her and smacked her into momentary submission. This was our first time witnessing Soho lashing out at Alex, but our sense was that this was not the first incident. Soon, we began to find cat urine outside the litter box on a regular basis. Next, I actually saw Alex urinate on clothing (if left on the floor), papers, decorative pillows, boxes, and one specific corner in the stairwell. Each day I went through the house searching for her spots and cleaning them as quickly as possible.

We took Alex to the vet to make sure that she did not have an infection, kidney disease, or a physical ailment. She did not. We tried pheromone plug-ins and other similar treatments. Nothing, short of leaving her outside all the time, worked. My husband, Ed, was tired of finding puddles and smells all over the house. I should have been tired too. But that cat wormed her way into my heart. She bonded with me right away, and she worked that bond. Ed could see how close I was to this cat, just as I had been with our previous cat, Biff, but reminded me that enough was enough. He even looked at me and said, "Alex is not the rebirth of Biff." At the time, I just thought this was a funny comment.

But I was not going to choose Alex over my husband. We found a cat rescue that would take cats in and, for a nice donation, let them live out their lives in peace. The day that we were scheduled to tale Alex to her new home, Ed had a change of heart. As difficult as she was, he worried about her well-being. He assured me that he would rather we deal with her than drop her off with strangers. Her troublesome behavior continued right up until the day after Soho died. Then, it was like flipping a switch. Alex stopped urinating in inappropriate places. It turned out that her problem was her bad blood with Soho.

Sometimes we have these special relationships with animals in our lives. I have loved each cat that has been a part of my life. Some relationships were deeper than others. With Biff, people looked at him and called him my familiar. Not in an insulting way, just in a recognition that we had an unusual human-feline closeness. I recall one friend looking at Biff and saying that when you looked into Biff's eyes, you saw an intelligent, knowing being looking back at you. I did not want a rebirth of Biff. I wanted him and all our other animal companions to move on. To be reborn as a cat again is not desirable.

We never knew where Alex came from. Because she had attached herself to me so quickly, we thought that perhaps she had lived with a woman. Maybe her previous human had died or had moved and left her behind. After Alex had lived with us for a while, we learned an interesting part of her story. When Alex came to our backyard, there were three women named Margaret living on the same block. One lived across the street from us and about five houses up. The other lived across the street and about two houses up. Through the course of friendly conversation and catch-up, I learned that the cat we named Alex had stopped at both of these women's homes. The first stop was at the house the farthest away. Alex stayed for a couple of days and then left on her own. The second stop was at the closer house. That Margaret (who went by Maggie) was uncertain about keeping her, but before she had to decide, Alex vanished. Alex crossed the street and came to my house, the home of the third Margaret. Alex might have visited every house on the block. Or was it her karma to live with a woman named Margaret?

Are our pets subject to rebirth? If you do not believe in rebirth, the quick answer is no. But if you are willing to consider some of the Buddhist teachings then, yes. We have looked at the Jātaka tales. These stories of the Buddha in his many past lives as a b*odhisatta* would indicate that not only are animals subject to rebirth, but we may have been animals in a past life.

Does this mean that the new puppy who actually chose you at the pet adoption fair is your favorite uncle reborn as a dog? Probably not. If this were the case, it would not be good for your uncle. An animal rebirth is less favorable than a human rebirth. When we learned that Ed was terminally ill, we jokingly created a plan where he would come back as a cat and then find me, and then if he had a good long life as a cat, it would be close to my life expectancy. In that way, we could both die and then be together again. This odd scenario allowed us to venture into the discussions we really needed to have about his death and our love and attachment for one another. Beyond that, it was not right view. The goal was not for Ed to come back as my next cat or to come back at all. The best outcome would be for him to have extinguished all of his karma and experience nirvana.

In the previous chapter, you read the passage that described how as the Buddha sat under the Bodhi tree meditating, he attained three forms of knowledge. The first was the ability to see his past lives. The second was to comprehend the entire system of karma and rebirth. He saw how those who lived immoral lives created negative karma, and that negative karma impacted their rebirths. Those who engaged in good conduct had positive rebirths. The Buddha realized that all sentient beings were part of the same system of karma and rebirth. From this realization came an understanding of the different realms of rebirth. The third knowledge he attained was the understanding of what causes our suffering and how we can release ourselves from our suffering. These are the Four Noble Truths:

1. There is suffering.//
2. Attachment and aversion cause this suffering.
3. There is a way out of suffering.
4. The way out is to live according to the Noble Eightfold Path.

It is how we deal with our suffering that leads us to engage in behaviors that build negative karma.

With this in mind, let's see how karma and rebirth are at play in the lives of our animal friends. We will start with the realms of rebirth, with a specific focus on the animal realm.

About the Animal Realm

In Buddhist cosmology, a being is born into a certain realm according to his, her, or their karma. You and I are in the human realm. Our realm and other realms are part of the four planes of existence, where rebirth takes place. Not all these planes are visible to humans. For example, we do not see beings who are in the "formless plane." From this life you may either experience nirvana, or you might be reborn as a human, an animal, a hungry ghost, a celestial being (deva), or some other form. Similarly, beings in other planes may come back as a human, an animal, a hungry ghost, a celestial being (deva) or some other form. The four planes are divided as follows:

1. *Kāmabhūmi* (plane of sense desire)
2. *Rūpabhūmi* (plane of form)
3. *Arūpabhūmi* (formless plane)
4. *Lokuttara* (supramundane)[1]

When we die, the best outcome is no rebirth. Otherwise, we come back according to the karma that we have accumulated.

In Buddhism, karma refers to actions and intentions: deeds you do and even thoughts that cross your mind. Your actions and thoughts, as influenced by your intentions, create karma. Karma is a complicated topic. In today's world, especially in the West, many see it as payback or retribution. We see too many bumper stickers and t-shirts that say, "Karma's a bitch." In our culture, there are not enough acknowledgments of good karma, and not enough recognition that "Instant Karma" might be a catchy song by John Lennon, but it is not an accurate representation of what we should expect in the real world. The karma that you experience is a blend of your past and current actions. You cannot go back in time and change anything about your current or past lives. The *Acintita Sutta* (AN 4.77) says, "There are these four unconjecturables that are not to be conjectured about, that would bring madness and vexation to anyone who conjectured about them."

The *sutta* goes on to state that the precise working out of the results of karma is one of the things we should not conjecture about. We are in the human realm because of our karma, and our pets are in the animal realm because of their karma. The human realm is within the *kāmabhūmi* (plane of sense desire). This plane is marked by our use of the five physical senses as a way to relate to the world. We use sight, hearing, touch, taste, and smell to interpret what is around us. We are subject to clinging and aversion by seeking more pleasant experiences and trying to avoid unpleasant experiences. While our default mode is sense desire, we do have the ability to meditate and experiences consciousness at the level of the plane of form.[2]

Within the *kāmabhūmi* are eleven realms. Seven are pleasurable, and four are unpleasurable. The human realm is one of the seven pleasurable or favorable destinations. The other six are dedicated to devas. Some may use the word *gods* or *deities*, but if you come from a Judeo-Christian background, these are not the same as God. Devas are not immortal, omniscient, or necessarily perfectly behaved. Devas can have what we would consider to be supernatural powers: invisibility to the human eye, ability to fly and transport themselves rapidly across great distances, and ability to transform into various shapes. None of these powers make them equivalent to a Buddha. A deva may live for thousands of years or more, but still, it is better to be a human.

In the *Pansu Sutta* (SN 56.102-113), this exchange occurs between the Buddha and some of his monks:

> What do you think, monks? Which is greater: the little bit of dust I have picked up with the tip of my fingernail, or the great earth?
>
> The great earth is far greater, lord. The little bit of dust the Blessed One has picked up with the tip of his fingernail is next to nothing. It doesn't even count. It's no comparison. It's not even a fraction, this little bit of dust the Blessed One has picked up with the tip of his fingernail, when compared with the great earth.
>
> In the same way, monks, few are the beings who, on passing away from the human realm, are reborn among human beings. Far more are the beings who, on passing away from the human realm, are reborn in hell.
>
> Therefore, your duty is the contemplation, "This is stress…This is the origination of stress…This is the cessation of stress." Your duty is the contemplation, "This is the path of practice leading to the cessation of stress."

The exchange continues in a similar vein. The Buddha explains that the number who are reborn in the human realm are few, and the number who are reborn in a hell realm, or as a hungry ghost or an animal, are far greater. More beings have difficult rebirths than have favorable rebirths. Even though in the *kāmabhūmi* there are seven realms that are good places for a rebirth, the four difficult realms have a much higher population. The animal realm is one of these. The other three are the *asura* realm, the hungry ghosts, and the hell realm. *Asuras* are a type of demon, perpetually unhappy and fighting with one another. Hungry ghosts, or *peta,* are always looking for sensual fulfillment. The hell realm is not like the hell as ruled by Lucifer. It is a place of great suffering, but it is not eternal suffering. None of these realms are permanent homes. Beings have finite life spans, even if they are very long lived, and they always have the potential to be reborn elsewhere.[3]

The animal realm is also referred to as *tiracchāna yoni*. And at the time of the Buddha, to say that someone was engaged in *tiracchānakatha* meant animal talk or idle chatter—a lowly form of discussion and behavior. Animals were used as food and to pull carts. They lived in a constant search for nourishment and safety from other beings and the elements. It may be hard for you to look at your well-loved pet and see a difficult rebirth, but remember the *tiracchāna yoni* is vast and includes all of the birds, reptiles, land creatures, water creatures, and insects.

Where you see your sweet dog, intelligent parrot, colorful fish, or sassy cat, there is also a being who is working on extinguishing some difficult karma. A being can be born into the animal realm as a result of performing unskillful bodily, verbal, or mental actions. How do you know what your companion did? You don't. And you do not need to know. We can turn to the *suttas* for some general guidance.

Per the *Saṁsappanīya sutta* (AN 10:216), someone who steals, lies, commits sexual misconduct, speaks harshly, speaks divisively, is covetous, or has cruel intentions is a person who is characterized as being creepy. These creepy, sneaky, crooked behaviors might land them, in the animal realm, and specifically as a creeping animal such as "snakes, scorpions, centipedes, mongooses, cats, mice, owls, or whatever other species of animal that creep away when they see humans."

For more, we can turn to the Bālapaṇḍita sutta (MN 129), where quite a few outcomes are predicted for those who are foolish, gluttonous and performs bad deeds:

> A fool who used to be a glutton here and did bad deeds here, when their body breaks up, after death, is reborn in the company of those sentient beings who feed on grass...And what animals feed on grass? Elephants, horses, cattle, donkeys, goats, deer, and various others.

The same statement regarding a fool who used to be a glutton and did bad deeds is repeated, and these animal rebirths are named as possible outcomes:

- After death is reborn in the company of those sentient beings who feed on dung. And what animals feed on dung?

    a. Chickens

    b. Pigs

    c. Dogs

    d. Jackals

e. and various others.

- After death is reborn in the company of those sentient beings who are born, live, and die in darkness. And what animals are born, live, and die in darkness?

  a. Moth

  b. Maggots

  c. Earthworms

  d. and various others.

- After death is reborn in the company of those sentient beings who are born, live, and die in water. And what animals are born, live, and die in water?

  a. Fish

  b. Turtles

  c. Crocodile

  d. and various others.

- After death is reborn in the company of those sentient beings who are born, live, and die in filth. And what animals are born, live, and die in filth? Those animals that are born, live, and die in a rotten fish, a rotten carcass, rotten porridge, or a sewer.

Some animal rebirths are more desirable. In the time of the Buddha, royal elephants were well tended and well fed. Dogs and birds may also have been royal pets. Mixed karma led to these animals returning into a better situation. When they died, they had a combination of right actions that helped them and some remaining negative karma that brought them to the animal realm. To return as a well-loved pet or a well-kept animal is an improvement.

What will happen to our pets when their current lives come to an end? Most likely, they will return to the animal realm. And most likely, they will return many, many times. James Stewart researched the opinions of current-day Buddhist monks to understand the plight of animals concerning rebirth and ultimate enlightenment. His *Journal of Buddhist Ethics article,* "Dharma Dogs: Can Animals Understand the Dharma? Textual and Ethnographic Considerations," contains his findings. Based on interviews and discussions with some Buddhist monks in Sri Lanka, he found, "The only way for animals to get out of such a situation is to expend the bad karma they have accumulated. This would be difficult to achieve when one considers the fact that many animals continue to act in morally impure ways by hunting and killing other creatures, thus only cementing their spiritual status."[4]

In the animal realm, it is more challenging to burn off karma. We have the advantage of access to the Dharma, spiritual teachers, and the ability to practice discernment. Animal consciousness is called *ahetuka,* "rootless" (AN-a 4:21). This term from the *Abhidhamma* means to be without certain mental factors, which are called *hetu,* or roots. The good news is that the unwholesome roots—greed, hatred, and delusion—are missing. The challenge is that the bright or wholesome roots—non-greed, non-hatred, and non-delusion—are also missing. As with a tree, a root helps to establish stability. The absence of the bright roots makes it harder to establish oneself in behaviors or mindsets that develop positive karma.

This state of rootlessness means that an animal goes through life experiencing the result of previous karma and has little ability or opportunity to make fresh karma. Escape from this realm is generally possible only as a result of old karma made in a higher birth coming to a delayed fruition. There are, however, exceptions to this rule. It is said that when animals such as deer or birds hear a Dharma talk or pay homage to the *saṅgha* or to a *cetiya* ("stupa," presumably by circumambulating it) they make skillful *kusala* (karma) whether they know it or not. [5]

Now, you may no longer use the expression "It's a dog's life" to describe a life of ease, and you likely have no desire to be a housecat or a hummingbird. But what you may wish is to find a way to help your furry, feathered, or scaly friend toward a better rebirth.

Is There No Escape?

Your beloved pet's spiritual journey can be a challenging concept to grasp, but it offers a unique opportunity for you to contemplate the cycle of karma and rebirth and accept these teachings in an open and nonjudgmental manner.

Do not forget about impermanence. Being in the animal realm for five hundred lifetimes or more is not the same as being there forever. How can our animal companions escape the *tiracchāna yoni?* We have already discussed that they need to burn off the karma that placed them there in the first place. And the way to accomplish this is the same as it is for you and me.

Learn and Practice the Dharma

It is hard for an animal to benefit from the Dharma. In fact, the *Saṅgīti sutta* (DN 33) lists nine lost opportunities for spiritual practice. Sariputta, one of the Buddha's senior monks, felt compelled to give this talk after observing a specific group suffering from infighting. He attributed their conflicts to lack of discipline and an inability to grasp the Buddha's teachings. And so, Sariputta took the opportunity to remind a group of monks of the key teachings, encouraging those present to recite the Dharma together. This *sutta* reminds us that being reborn in the animal realm is one of these nine lost opportunities for spiritual practice. The relevant passage reads:

> A Realized One has arisen in the world. He teaches the Dharma leading to peace, extinguishment, awakening, as proclaimed by the Holy One...But a person has been reborn in the animal realm. This is the second lost opportunity for spiritual practice.

The challenge is that most animals are not capable of listening to and comprehending the Dharma. But *most* is not the same thing as *all*. There are stories of animals being present during teachings, and those animals benefited. Consider this passage from the *Dhammapada:*

> When the Buddha taught the devas in Tāvatiṃsa (a Deva realm) daily for an entire rainy season, each afternoon he would return

to earth and pass on the synopsis of the teaching to Sāriputta. These became the seven books of the Abhidhamma and Sāriputta first taught these to a select group of five hundred bhikkhu disciples. They had all been.

Small bats living in a cave at the time of Kassapa Buddha. As they hung from the ceiling of the cave, two bhikkhus were reciting the Abhidhamma aloud as they did walking meditation. The bats grasped a sign in the sound of the bhikkhus' voices.

They did not understand the meaning, "these are the aggregates, these are the elements etc." but simply by grasping the sign after death they were reborn in a deva world. They remained enjoying the bliss of a deva existence for the entire period between Buddhas and were then reborn as householders in Sāvatthi during the time of Gotama Buddha. (Dhp-a 14:2) [6]

Even though animals do not understand the teachings, they may still derive benefit from hearing them. And that can lead to a rebirth outside of the animal realm, and then eventually to a rebirth in the human realm.

Do Good Deeds

Performing a task or sending good intentions to others, without expecting anything in return generates good karma, and helps to burn off negative karma. When James Stewart discussed animals and their potential rebirth with some Sri Lankan monks, one of the monks suggested that perhaps animals can have a better rebirth by engaging in good deeds.[7]

The next logical question is "How can an animal do a good deed?" Most of the time, these good deeds require help from compassionate humans. Kalupitiya, a monk who spoke with Stewart gave this example:

> During the annual Kandy procession (*esala pĕrahara*) a special elephant carries the sacred tooth relic through the streets to be displayed to devoted attendees. According to Sinhala Buddhist tradition, the sacred tooth is one of the few remaining relics of the Buddha and is therefore an object of intense veneration. Merely viewing the relic is considered a meritorious deed. The great royal elephant (*7laja attha*) and other animals who have lifted the sacred tooth (*daḷadā dat*) can receive merit.
>
> Kalupitiya is making the case that the act of carrying the tooth relic is a good deed. It does not matter what the elephant understands. [8]

You can help your animal friends by placing them in situations where they can be helpful to others. Bring your dog on a visit to someone who loves dogs but is unable to have a dog of their own. Allow a young neighbor or family member to learn responsibility by caring for and feeding your pet. Be on the lookout for situations where your animal friend is able to interact with others in a positive manner. Then place your animal friend in a position to bring value.

Participate in Regular Observances

There is a story in the *Vinaya* that tells of a *nāga* (a being that is half human and half serpent) who uses magic to appear as a human and then joins the Buddha's monks. The Buddha realizes what has happened and casts him out. He reprimands him, "You, serpent, go away, observe the Observance Day (*poya*), precisely on the fourteenth, fifteenth, and eighth day of the half month. Thus, you will be freed quickly from birth as a serpent and get back to human status" (Vin-MV 1 111). The Buddha is telling the *nāga* that there is no shortcut to the human realm. The path is a consistent and dedicated spiritual practice.

Poya is the name used in Sri Lanka to refer to the days of the month for special Buddhist practice. You may also hear the term *Uposattha*. The day of the full moon is a special day for Buddhist practice, as is the day of the new moon and, in some Theravāda countries (like Thailand), the quarter moon days. These special days for observance were in place for the religions in existence at the time of the Buddha and were adopted by his followers, and they are still in place today. [9]

I meditate with a group who meets online on special practice days. Because I am joining from home, it is possible for my cats to be part of our meditation and discussion. I would not force either cat to sit in the room with me, but if one or both of them are present, they may reap the benefit of participating in regular observances.

Spend Time with Monks or around Buddhist Relics and Sites

Animals who are able to spend time in close proximity with monks or near Buddhist relics and holy Buddhist sites can experience a positive impact on their karma. This is true for us as well. The opportunity to be near beings who are more advanced in their practice is like an energetic boost. The same can be true of holy places. If you can, bring your pet with you to the local Buddhist temple, or with you to listen to a respected monk or nun speak.

Animals Who Broke Free

If you were an animal at the time of the Buddha and in some way assisted him, it is possible that this would earn you a better rebirth. This is rumored to be true of his horse and of a monkey and an elephant who were attendants to the Buddha.

When the Buddha left his father's home in his quest to overcome old age, sickness, and death, he rode away on his horse, Kanthaka. Once he reached a certain distance from his family home, he sent Kanthaka back. Legend has it that soon after, Kanthaka died of heartbreak, and for his service, he was reborn in a deva realm.

After he rode away from his father's home, the Buddha spent six years wandering and looking for the path to enlightenment. During the rainy season he went on retreat. He spent one such retreat in the forest. It happened that an elephant named Pālileyyaka, determined to live alone, had left his herd, and he found the Buddha in the forest under a tree. Pālileyyaka used a branch from the tree as a broom and swept the area clean. He also fetched water and gathered fruit for the Buddha to eat. Pālileyyaka followed the Buddha to the outskirts of the village and carried his bowl for him. When the Buddha returned from the village, once again Pālileyyaka carried his things. At night, the kindly elephant kept other wild animals away so that the Buddha could sleep safely.

Seeing the elephant serving the Buddha inspired a monkey. The monkey brought the Buddha some honeycomb. At first, the Buddha would not eat the honeycomb. The monkey realized that this was because there were larvae in the honeycomb. The monkey picked out all of the larvae and offered the honeycomb again. This time, the Buddha accepted it, and the monkey was overjoyed, dancing and jumping from tree branch to tree branch. Unfortunately, he fell to his death, but his reward was a rebirth in the deva realm called Tāvatiṃsa. And Pālileyyaka? He died of a broken heart when the Buddha ended his rain retreat and left the forest. He, too, was rewarded for his service with a rebirth in Tāvatiṃsa.

The above examples show that it is possible for our animal friends to move forward. The stories also reinforce the idea that animals have more work to do to release negative karma and create positive karma. Another important lesson is that we should seek to behave in a way that will never lead to our rebirth in the animal realm. We should only seek to conduct ourselves with the highest moral standards and to work toward extinguishing our karma.

You Can Help

We do not live during a time when there is a Buddha available, so you cannot volunteer your pet as an assistant. You might not be able to enlist your pet to help carry a Buddhist relic. You might not live near a holy site or even have access to a group of monks (although if you do, bring your pet with you as visit the site, or ask the monks if there is a day when they provide blessings to animals). As for the Dharma, you can expose your pet to the Dharma. I am not recommending you take your boa constrictor to your meditation group without first checking in with your community members, but you can meditate with your pet next to you or take them on a walking meditation. You can read the *suttas* out loud within earshot or play recordings of chanting.

In terms of helping with good deeds, when you provide a loving and peaceful home, your pet is less likely to be involved in fighting and violence. On the one hand, when you keep animals in your home and away from their natural surroundings, it can be seen as restrictive and against their way. It can also keep them from killing or being killed, from terrorizing or being terrorized. My cats that lie indoors are not chasing and killing birds, lizards, and other creatures. This is to their benefit. If you have a pet that is able to act as a service or emotional support animal, that animal is doing a good deed. If your pet is calm and well behaved enough, perhaps (with permission), visit the elderly or another group who would benefit from interacting with a friendly creature.

Will any of these activities make a difference? I cannot promise you that your boa constrictor will be reborn as a deva. But your spiritual devotion is not going to hurt. And you know who it is helping? You!

End Notes

[1] Punna Dhammo, "THE BUDDHIST COSMOS," n.d., page 144.
[2] Dhammo.
[3] "The Thirty-One Planes of Existence," accessed August 6, 2023, https://www.accesstoinsight.org/ptf/dhamma/sagga/loka.html.
[4] James Stewart, "Dharma Dogs: Can Animals Understand the Dharma? Textual and Ethnographic Considerations," n.d., page 56.
[5] Dhammo, "THE BUDDHIST COSMOS.", page 237.
[6] Dhammo., page 238.
[7] Stewart, "Dharma Dogs: Can Animals Understand the Dharma? Textual and Ethnographic Considerations," 53.
[8] Stewart, "Dharma Dogs: Can Animals Understand the Dharma? Textual and Ethnographic Considerations.", page 53.
[9] Stewart., page 50.

Chapter 4

Animals Appearing in *Suttas*

The teachings in the Pāli canon are vast. Some current-day collections of these teachings are fifty printed volumes. The good news is that if you would like to study the Pāli canon, you have plenty of source material. You can really immerse yourself. The bad news? Well, there is no bad news because time spent with the *suttas* is time well spent.

Together we have explored the Jātaka tales, how the Buddha lived in past lives as an animal, and how some of his disciples have also lived past lives as an animal. It is easy to make the connection that we, too, have had past lives as animals. With 547 stories of differing lengths, the journey from *Bodhisattva* to Buddha was a long one.

The Jātakas represent just one area of the Pāli canon. Animals also feature in teachings outside of the Jātakas. They might be working animals or used to describe human behaviors, or perhaps they play an active part in a story. We have read stories where animals teach us moral behavior.

Our understanding of our pets and other animals as part of our spiritual lives cannot be complete without looking at how animals fit into society at the time of the Buddha. In day-to-day living, how much thought did people give to the life of a monkey compared to the life of a human? How much compassion and consideration was a human really expected to give to a deer? And what were humans supposed to eat?

You might be wondering, "But what does that have to do with our world now?" Overall, the teachings contain some messages that are just as relevant today. We still make decisions about the lives of the animals sharing the world with us. What is the best way for us to coexist?

By looking at the rules the Buddha created for his monks and nuns, you will see animals are important but not more important than humans. Buddhists hold non-human sentient beings in high regard. Everyday creatures, as contrasted to the more whimsical or magical inhabitants of the Jātaka tales, can still model admirable qualities and moral behavior. And yet, sometimes they are food.

By looking at the teachings presented here, you will find a balanced view—not a perfect solution, but potentially a way for you to reconcile your life with your pet and your relationships with other animals as you consider how to advance on your spiritual path.

Animals and the Rules of Conduct

As the Buddha traveled and shared his teachings, men joined him, creating a community of monks. Eventually, they allowed women to join (living in their own separate community). As the groups grew in size, it became necessary to create rules to ensure harmonious living and to help monks and nuns stay true to the Buddha's teaching. These rules of conduct are the

Pāṭimokkha. In the Pāli canon, the *Pāṭimokkha* is part of the *Vinaya Tipiṭaka*, or the "Basket of Discipline."

In the Jātaka tales, the line between humans and animals is often blurred. Animals are depicted as thinking and speaking. When the animals are representing the past lives of humans, they are very different from the monkeys, crocodiles, or deer of our natural world. [1] In the *suttas*, animals are definitely spiritually inferior. They are not to be ordained, and there is a rule against even reciting the *Pāṭimokkha* in front of an animal. [2] This might seem absurd to you. Who would try to ordain an animal? The Buddha developed the *Pāṭimokkha* over time. As a challenging situation arose, he considered it and, when appropriate, created a rule. So yes, someone tried to ordain an animal.

The first precept is to abstain from killing. This is true of the five precepts, the extended eight precepts that some Buddhist practioners follow on special days of practice and on retreat, the precepts that novice monks and nuns follow, and the precepts ordained monks and nuns follow. The *Vinaya* categorizes animal lives differently than human lives. Animals are not just spiritually inferior; their lives do not have the same value. Consider the punishment that comes with breaking the first precept. The taking of a human life is one of the highest offenses. It is punishable by immediate expulsion from the order. A monk or nun who takes a human life is disrobed. The taking of an animal life is a lesser offense, requiring confession and possibly an act of penance. [3]

In another rule regarding the treatment of animals, we can see that animals are to be treated well, and they should not be harmed or killed, but if they are, it is not the most severe offense that can be committed. One of the rules states that if a monk or nun digs a pit and an animal falls into that pit and dies, this is an offense that requires atonement. If the animal survives, even if injured, the monk or nun are guilty of wrongdoing, but no further action or discipline is required. [4]

Animals are considered to be the property of others. A monk or nun who takes an animal for their own purposes is breaking the second precept of abstaining from taking what is not given. If that monk or nun has the intention of freeing the animal because they believe the animal is suffering, then it is a lesser offense. The offense is that someone else's property has been breached. [5]

According to these rules and the principles of karma and rebirth, a hierarchy of sentient beings emerges. Humans are the most spiritually advanced and the most important sentient beings. We have been born into the most desirable realm, a realm where we can practice the Dharma and reach enlightenment. This does not make it acceptable to purposefully bring harm to others. In fact, as more spiritually advanced beings, we have a responsibility to treat all others with respect and compassion. We are not an entitled ruling class. The right view is one of guardianship. We are in a position of power, and it is our responsibility to wield that power skillfully.

We are to abstain from killing sentient beings. But killing a human is a greater offense than killing an animal. Remember, the fact that one crime carries a lesser penalty than another crime does not mean we opt to commit the lesser crime. Our goal is to commit no crime at all.

Suttas: A Broader Context

While the *Vinaya* provides context for the relationship between humans and animals and sets down the rules for the monks and nuns, the *suttas* have teachings that are relevant to all of us. Laypeople interacted with animals differently. Animals were part of the economic system. Oxen pulled carts or plows; deer and fish were a source of food. Animals were sold and traded. What additional guidelines were provided so that a person could live as a productive member of society and advance on their spiritual path? The *suttas* are where we turn our attention to gain insight into how to skillfully live alongside our animal companions. It is in these teachings that we find animals used as similes, warnings against acting as an animal, and metaphors to help us comprehend mindfulness.

Sometimes, when the Buddha or one of his disciples taught, only monks were present to hear him. Other times local community members were present. Today, we have the ability to study these teachings no matter who was present during the original discourse. After his death, the Buddha's disciples contained to share his teachings. The recitation of the *suttas* was not restricted to monks and nuns. That means that we can turn to these teachings to guide us. In the *Kulāvaka Sutta,* we find reinforcement of the reminder to avoid killing animals. The story tells of a battle between devas and demons. The devas have lost and the demons are pursuing them to finalize their victory. As the devas flee, it becomes clear that between them and safety are some nesting birds. They risk losing everything just to avoid disturbing nesting birds. This passage tells the story:

> Once upon a time, mendicants, a battle was fought between the

gods and the demons. In that battle the demons won and the gods lost. Defeated, the gods fled north with the demons in pursuit.

Then Sakka, lord of gods, addressed his charioteer Mātali in verse:
"Mātali, don't ram the bird nests
in the red silk-cotton woods with your chariot pole.
I'd rather give up our lives to the demons
than deprive these birds of their nests."

"Yes, lord," replied Mātali. And he turned the chariot back around, with its team of a thousand thoroughbreds.

Then the demons thought, "Now Sakka's chariot has turned back. The demons will have to fight the gods a second time!" Terrified, they retreated right away to the citadel of the demons.

And that's how Sakka came to win victory by principle. (SN 11)

By looking out for the birds, Sakka won a battle where the odds were definitely against him. He and his warriors reaped an immediate reward. The message seems clear: show compassion to other living beings, and you will benefit. It seems likely that in this battle, they killed and harmed one another. It is as if this harm to one another elevates the importance of non-harm to weaker beings. The birds are not able to defend themselves. They are not meant to be part of this war. What does this teach us about our responsibility to smaller, weaker species?

Sakka and his warriors see immediate positive results. Sometimes the benefits come later. For example, when elephants know that a beloved human caretaker has died, they will travel great distances to pay their respects. How they knew is still a mystery. In one instance, an elephant gathered grass and flowers and placed them on the grave of one of her caretakers.[6] It seems like some kind of a spiritual symbiosis has taken place.

The *suttas* depict animals that have been mistreated or killed. Animals are part of a king's wealth, and even a monarch who has reached spiritual attainment has animals at his command and uses skins of dead animals as a show of his wealth and power. In the *Mahāsudassana sutta* (DN 17), we have King Mahasudassana, who is discussed as traversing the four jhanas and practiced loving kindness, and yet he has "eighty-four thousand elephants adorned with gold ornaments, with gold banners and spread with gold nets...eighty-four thousand carriages, covered with lion-skins, tiger-skins, leopard-skins or with orange-colored cloth, adorned with gold ornaments, gold banners and spread with gold nets."

On the one hand, King Mahasudassana is skilled on the path. He has obtained the highest level of meditative concentration. Yet he has had animals killed for his own display. It shows the disconnect between wealth and privilege and spirituality. In today's world we may not have carriages covered with animal skins and armies of elephants, but we are not without our own materialistic equivalents: fancy cars, designer clothing, and assistants, chefs, and housekeepers. The actual teaching point of this particular *sutta* is impermanence: eventually all the things and lands owned by the king disappear. For us, it is a reminder not to let our concept of status get in the way of our responsibility to our animal friends. You might reach a certain level of status and wealth and think that means that you need to have a fancy breed of dog or cat or acquire an exotic animal as a pet. But there are plenty of animals waiting in the shelters for good homes. Instead of one fancy pedigreed pet, how about adopting two pets of an unknown breed? Maybe send some money to help spay and neuter strays.

In the time of the Buddha, people and animals had more interactions. Today, you can get in your car and drive to work without seeing other non-human beings. There was a time when seeing an animal was unavoidable. Oxen pulled carts. People milked cows at markets. Stray dogs roamed the streets, and monkeys ate fruit in the trees above. This made it easier to use animals to teach desirable and undesirable qualities. These are not past-life stories like the Jātakas. These are animal references to teach specific ideas. The animals are not anthropomorphized. Certain aspects of these animals' temperaments are as teaching devices. In the *Anguttara Nikaya*, there are multiple passages using colts, horses, and thoroughbred horses to describe kinds of people. In AN 9.22 there are three kinds of colts, three kinds of horses, and three kinds of thoroughbred horses. For each, there is:

1. One that possesses speed but not beauty or the right proportions.

2. One that possesses speed and beauty but not the right proportions.

3. One that has speed, beauty, and the right proportions.

You might suspect that the colt represents someone who is the least advanced on the path and the thoroughbred is the most advanced. You are correct. This is how it maps out:

- Colt – Speed represents the cause of suffering.

- Regular Horse – Speed represents the destruction of the five lower fetters.

- Thoroughbred – Speed represents the recoginition that liberation has been reached.

For each type of horse, beauty represents understanding the Dharma and living with discipline. To possess the right proportions means to become ordained. All horses are valuable sentient beings. Like the horses, we are all in different stages in our Buddhist practice. We will meet colts, regular horses, and thoroughbreds. If we incorporate this idea with the concept of our pets and animal companions and their spiritual paths, they, too, are in different stages. Because we are human, we might want to make assumptions about others: "Oh, ignore her, she isn't even a colt yet." That is not the way. Move forward with an awareness that we are all on our own journeys. And as you live with your furry, feathered, or scaly friends, think about how you can meet them where they are. And know that your ability to help them is directly linked to your own growth.

Once you understand the Second Noble Truth of Suffering, you can work to recognize clinging and aversion within yourself. What do you think that means in terms of how you interact with your pets and other animals? At a minimum, if you can love the creatures around you with respect and an understanding of impermanence, knowing that your lifespan is probably longer, you can create a relationship that is less codependent.

If you destroy the five lower fetters—if you stop clinging to a defining self-identity, get rid of uncertainty in the Dharma, stop being owned by sensual desire and ill will, and avoid grasping at your Buddhist practice—imagine the clarity with which you can live your life. How might this translate into how you care for other creatures? In what way would greater clarity help you make decisions from pure intentions and create outcomes that benefit your animal friends?

Analogies discussing animals can be skillful teaching devices, yet we are not meant to be animals. The teaching with the colt, the regular horse, and the thoroughbred is not telling us to be horses. There is a story about two monks who pretended to be animals as part of their Buddhist practice. Punna, who was a friend of Seniya, went to the Buddha and asked what would become of Seniya. It seemed that Seniya was engaged in practicing as a dog. He ate scraps like a dog, and he ate on the floor like a dog. When he listened to the Buddha teach, he curled up to his side like a dog.

At first, the Buddha put Punna off, telling him not to ask about Seniya and his dog practice. But Punna persisted. And the Buddha gave him an answer:

Here, Punna, someone develops the dog duty fully and unstintingly, he develops the dog-habit fully and unstintingly, he develops the dog mind fully and unstintingly, he develops dog behavior fully and unstintingly. Having done that, on the dissolution of the body, after death, he reappears in the company of dogs. But if his view is such as this: "By this virtue or duty or asceticism or religious life I shall become a (great) god or some (lesser) god," that is wrong view in his case. Now there are two destinations for one with wrong view, I say: hell, or the animal womb. So, Punna, if his dog duty is perfected, it will lead him to the company of dogs; if it is not, it will lead him to hell. (MN 57)

The message is clear: if you act like an animal, you will experience the karma of an animal. Your learning comes from thinking about animals, not thinking you are an animal. Most of us do not pretend to be animals. Most of us benefit from establishing restraint and mindfulness.

In the *Chappana Sutta,* animals represent the ways in which a monk can be distracted, and advice is given on how to tame those animals or dwell in focused concentration. In this sutta, the Buddha describes distractions as six animals. Each is a different size and strength and attracted to their own environment. There is a crocodile, a bird, a dog, a hyena, a monkey, and a snake. In this metaphor, a person attaches all of these animals together with one strong rope. This passage describes what happens next:

> Just as if a person, catching six animals of different ranges of different habitats, were to bind them with a strong rope. Catching a snake, he would bind it with a strong rope. Catching

a crocodile…a bird…a dog…a hyena…a monkey, he would bind it with a strong rope. Binding them all with a strong rope, and tying a knot in the middle, he would set chase to them.

Then those six animals of different ranges of different habitats, would each pull toward its own range and habitat. The snake would pull, thinking, "I'll go into the anthill." The crocodile would pull, thinking, "I'll go into the water." The bird would pull, thinking, "I'll fly up into the air." The dog would pull, thinking, "I'll go into the village." The hyena would pull, thinking, "I'll go into the charnel ground." The monkey would pull, thinking, "I'll go into the forest." And when these six animals became internally exhausted, they would submit, they would surrender, they would come under the sway of whichever among them was the strongest. (SN 35.206)

In the above excerpt, exhaustion does not represent a calm and focused mind; it really means that our senses drag us back and forth during our meditation. The animals are our senses: the eye, the ear, the nose, the tongue, the body and the intellect. We bounce around toward something appealing to look at or toward good tastes and pleasant sounds. Whichever sensation has the biggest draw, that is where our concentration lands.

The *sutta* continues and explains that if those six animals were captured, tied up with a rope, and attached to a firm stake or post, then as much as they would pull, they would be anchored by that post. They would eventually just sit next to that post. This is an excellent analogy of what it feels like to practice mindfulness. Some days, you sit in meditation, and it seems like every five seconds your mind wanders off to thinking about work, your friends, your partner, or a movie that you just watched. You have all these animals attached to you and pulling your mind in every direction. But you keep practicing. You become more secure in your practice, and all those animals are still with you, but you are able to acknowledge them and keep them in place. If you learn to develop mindfulness immersed in the body, then you have restraint. The post is mindfulness. When the post is set, your foundation is set, and your senses will not take control.

Elephants, Deer, Lions, and Jackals

Before we leave animal representations behind, let's take a quick look at a few other animals. These short passages help us to understand the perceptions that people had regarding other animals in their midst. And these perceptions communicated certain conditions, such as a concentrated mind, peace, or fearfulness.

Elephants

Elephants are usually depicted in a positive light. A tamed elephant reminds us of a calm mind, and an enraged elephant represents an uncontrolled mind. The *Sagathavagga* compares a monk who has attained perfect calm to a tamed elephant (SN I 141).

The *Theragatha* (poems and enlightenment stories of monks) uses the image of the elephant in battle as a model of mindfulness. The monk Vijitasena was born into a family of elephant trainers. In his poem (Tha 355-7), he likened restraining the mind to keeping back elephants at the gate. He threatened his wandering mind that he would turn it back under control like the trainer who firmly wields his hook and makes the untamed elephant turn against its will.

In the *Therigatha* (poems and enlightenment stories of nuns), the nun Dantika uses thoughts of a tamed elephant obeying the driver's orders as a motivation for calming and training her mind (Thi 48-50).

Deer

Deer are gentle in nature and generally project a positive image. Often an accomplished monk is compared to a deer, as in, "the recluse dwells in the forest free of fear and anxiety, with the heart of that of a deer." The deer is "unconcerned, unruffled, abiding in a state of no expectations." [7]

The *Samandaka Samyutta* (SN 39) tells the recluse to be independent like a deer. A deer is not tethered and can wander the forest and pastures as it likes. And in describing who he lived with before he reached enlightenment, the Buddha stated that he avoided humans, just like a deer in the forest flees when it sees a man. [8]

There are occasions where the cautious nature of the deer is framed in a negative light. One sutta tells of a recluse who has become so disenchanted with gossip that he was like a deer who was afraid of the wind in the forest.[9]

Lions

The Buddha's lion roar on impermanence is said to be so powerful that it causes all who hear it to quake and tremble. The lion is a strong and majestic creature. The symbolism is not hard to comprehend. Even those of us who have only seen a lion in the zoo understand the strength of this beast. Perhaps we have read or heard stories that describe the lion as the King of the Jungle. Today's lions in the wild do not live in the jungle, but there was a time when they did inhabit the forested lands of other countries. Lions also represent bravery. "Bhikkhus, there are these two that are not terrified by a bursting thunderbolt. What two? A bhikkhu whose taints are destroyed and a lion, king of the beasts. These are the two that are not terrified by a bursting thunderbolt." (AN 2:59)

A monk with established spiritual attainments and a lion are equal in bravery.

The lion is also one of the symbols used for the Buddha (or Tathagata):

> The lion, bhikkhus, is a designation for the Tathagata, the Arahant, the Perfectly Enlightened One...when the Tathagata teaches the Dhamma to an assembly, this is his lion's roar.
>
> 1. If the Tathagata teaches the Dhamma to *bhikkhus*, he teaches it respectfully, not disrespectfully.
>
> 2. If the Tathagata teaches the Dhamma to *bhikkhunis*...
>
> 3. To male lay followers...
>
> 4. To female lay followers, he teaches it respectfully, not disrespectfully.
>
> 5. If the Tathagata teaches the Dhamma to worldlings, even to food-carriers and hunters, he teaches it respectfully, not disrespectfully. For what reason? Because the Tathagata has respect for the Dhamma, reverence for the Dhamma." (AN 5.99)

Like the Buddha when he teaches, the lion treas his environment with respect and treats his prey with respect.

Jackals

The jackal gets no respect. In the *Sagathavagga Sutta* (SN I 66), we learn that in spite of its howl, the jackal is a wretched beast never equal to the lion. The teachings consistently depict the jackal as dishonest and disreputable. It is hard to find a kind word for the jackal. [10]

Animal Welfare and Vegetarianism

The Buddha lived in a time when an entire religion practiced animal sacrifice. Actually, so do we. It is not as common, but some countries and traditions still practice animal sacrifice. The Buddha spoke out against animal sacrifice. The passage below shares his response to his monks when, after returning from alms rounds, he learned that the locals were engaging in a great slaughter of animals for their ruler, King Pasenadi:

> Horse sacrifice, human sacrifice, the sacrifices of the "casting of the yoke-pin" the "royal soma drinking," and the "unbarred"—these huge violent sacrifices yield no great fruit.
>
> The great sages of good conduct don't attend sacrifices where goats, sheep, and cattle and various creatures are killed.
>
> But the great sages of good conduct do attend non-violent sacrifices of regular family tradition, where goats, sheep, and cattle, and various creatures aren't killed.
>
> A clever person should sacrifice like this, for this sacrifice is very fruitful. For a sponsor of sacrifices like this, things get better, not

worse. Such a sacrifice is truly abundant, and even the deities are pleased. (SN 3.9)

Some interpret this to mean that the killing of the animals was not the problem; it simply is not an effective way to advance in your spiritual practice. Other passages mention using oils, rice, and other items as non-violent sacrifices in place of animal sacrifice. These are fruitful sacrifices.

These short passages from the Dhammapada remind us of the overall guidance of treating all sentient beings with respect. Animal sacrifices violate the rights of other sentient beings and are inappropriate ways to attain spiritual growth.

> All tremble at violence; all fear death. Putting oneself in the place of another, one should not kill nor cause another to kill.
>
> All tremble at violence; life is dear to all. Putting oneself in the place of another, one should not kill nor cause another to kill.
>
> One who, while himself seeking happiness, oppresses with violence other beings who also desire happiness, will not attain happiness hereafter.
>
> One who, while himself seeking happiness, does not oppress with violence other beings who also desire happiness, will find happiness hereafter. (Dhp X 129-132)

In a later chapter, we'll delve more deeply into the idea of guardianship. We are caretakers of this planet and its ecosystems. Like the devas who battled the demons, we want to be respectful of the animal lives around us. We do not want to wipe out other creatures due to a lack of caring or a lack of awareness. In our recent history we used animals to test cosmetics, medicines, and other items. While animal testing has become widely disparaged and banned in many places, it does still occur. We train animals to handle dangerous situations to prevent the loss of human life. Think of bomb sniffing dogs, or police dogs. We still ride horses, mules, elephants, and camels. And we eat animal flesh.

This brings us to the issue of vegetarianism. Are all Buddhists vegetarian? Did the Buddha tell us to be vegetarians? The *suttas* and the *Vinaya* teach us not to harm others, not to kill others, while also prioritizing human life over animal life. Ranking higher in the hierarchy does not make it appropriate to subjugate animals, so does that mean there is no reaching enlightenment if you eat meat? Not exactly. I am not going to be able to give you clear guidance. As a species, humans tend to be omnivores. We eat plants and meat. Many of us also have a choice. We have a food supply that does not force toward one specific diet.

The Buddha is said to have reached enlightenment and upon his death entered nirvana, not to return. That same Buddha ate meat when it was given to him during alms rounds. Some may find it more than a touch ironic that the Buddha is reported to have died from eating tainted meat. That does not simplify the issue. You can take the perspective that meat killed him, and yet he transcended.

At a high level, the issue of whether or not to be a vegetarian can be attributed to differences between Theravāda and Mahāyāna ways of thinking. I have heard multiple Theravāda teachers state that the Buddha never said be a vegetarian. The Buddha told his monks and nuns not to engage in the killing of animals for food and not to eat an animal that was killed just for their meal. To this day when monks go on alms rounds or food is donated, the prevailing wisdom is to eat what is given. From a Theravāda Buddhist perspective, you are not required to be vegetarian. However, the Mahāyāna interpretation is that monks and nuns are definitely vegetarian, and most likely vegan. Laypeople might not be required to be as strict with their diets.

The overarching guideline is to remember that we are to be compassionate toward all sentient beings and to refrain from harming or killing any sentient being.

Before we continue, remember that for the most part, I am sharing with you Theravāda teachings. The *suttas* I bring you come from the Pāli canon. I am not a vegetarian. This does not mean that I do not see the challenges we face when it comes to eating animals.

We have already discussed that the Pāli canon warns against causing harm or taking the lives of other sentient beings. We know that the animals we eat are sentient beings. Still, the teachings that directly apply this to the eating of animal flesh tend to come from Mahāyāna texts.

The teachings in the Pāli canon can absolutely make a case against the eating of meat. Or you can rely on passages such as the *sutta* to Jīvaka.

> Jīvaka Komārabhacca went to the Blessed One and, on arrival, having bowed down to him, sat to one side. As he was sitting there, he said to the Blessed One, "Lord, I have heard it said that "They slaughter animals for the sake of Gotama the

contemplative. Gotama the contemplative knowingly eats the meat prepared for his sake in dependence on that action."

In the passage above, Jīvaka is asking if some people who host the Buddha and give him food are having animals killed specifically for the Buddha's meals. This is problematic since the Buddha has been teaching non-violence toward animals and tells his disciples not to encourage animal slaughter for them. In this instance, detractors of the Buddha are trying to spread rumors. The Buddha replies to Jīvaka,

> Jīvaka, those who say, "They slaughter animals for the sake of Gotama the contemplative. Gotama the contemplative knowingly eats the meat prepared for his sake in dependence on that action": They are not speaking in line with what I have said, and they are slandering me with what is unfactual.

In advising Jīvaka the Buddha reminds him of three conditions under which meat is not to be consumed, and then three conditions under which meat may be consumed,

> I say that there are three instances in which meat should not be consumed: when it is seen, heard, or suspected [that the animal was killed for one's sake]. These are the three instances in which I say that meat should not be consumed.
>
> I say that there are three instances in which meat may be consumed: when it is not seen, not heard, and not suspected. These are the three instances in which I say that meat may be consumed. (MN 55)

The *sutta* also states that if a layperson finds and slaughters an animal just for the purpose of feeding the Buddha or one of monks, that layperson will experience demerit. If the meat is not purposefully killed for the Buddha or his monks, and if the meat can be eaten with no wish of harm or suffering to the animal and a loving kindness meditation has been performed toward the village and toward the people and the animals within, there is no harm.

Where does this leave us? Most of us do not send compassion to the entire system from which our food originates before we eat. There is also the problem of knowing whether or not the meat was killed for us. If I buy a package of chicken in the grocery story, was the chicken killed for me? If all of us stopped buying chicken, there would be no chicken in the store. And I am not going to reach for the loophole that nobody selected a specific chicken and killed it on my behalf.

Another challenge is that the Noble Eightfold Path encourages us to engage in Right Livelihood. Raising meat to be killed and killing animals for food are not considered to be right livelihood:

> Bhikkhus, a lay follower should not engage in these five trades. What five? Trading in weapons, trading in living beings, trading in meat, trading in intoxicants, and trading in poisons. (AN 5:177)

Where does the meat come from? Once, on a trip to India, my colleague and I went shopping. He found a leather jacket that he really liked. As he was contemplating buying it, he looked at the shop owner and said, "I thought you weren't supposed to kill cows." And with a deadpan expression, the shop owner said, "I didn't. Someone else did, and now it is in my store." That's cheating in a system where cheating does not move you ahead.

The challenge is not just what we eat; it is what we wear, what we carry, what we sit on, and what we use to keep warm. You can wear or use vegan leather. You can buy previously owned clothing and shoes. In that way, you are not supporting the killing of additional animals.

Take a look around your home. How many items do you have that came from an animal? And what level of pain or suffering was inflicted? I am not asking you to do this to feel shame or guilt. You can consider this an opportunity to reflect on what you eat and use as you move forward and to develop your own compassion meditation or mantra to extend toward the animal world. In this way if you eat meat, you can do so with more awareness and loving kindness. If you do not eat meat, you can still send compassion and loving kindness to the animals who are impacted by your presence in their world.

Perhaps what James McDermott asserts in "Animals and Humans in Early Buddhism," is true. The Buddha did not believe that our purification or freedom from suffering came from what we ate but from our restraint.[11] It came from our ability to follow the middle way, meaning abstaining from self-indulgence and also self-denial—living in this world in a way that you do not tend toward clinging or aversion. And that the choices you make, the actions you take, and the thoughts you nurture come from a place of pure intention. In this way, you cease to create karma. I leave you to make your own observations and decisions.

An Imperfect World

After reading a sampling of the *suttas* that deal with animals and considering the guidelines that monks and nuns follow with regard to animals, it occurs to me that when it comes to the role of animals, I see similarities between early Buddhist times and today. There is an overall expectation of treating our animal friends with compassion and respect. And there is an understanding that we do not always do so.

Both of my cats came to me because a friend of mine was fostering them for a local cat rescue. In the past, other cats came to my door as strays. A wise family member once said, "When the time is right, a cat will present itself." Taking in homeless cats has always felt like the right thing to do. The challenge is how many can I rescue? There are many more kittens who need homes, who will have shorter, more difficult lives on the street or face euthanasia in a shelter. And yet, I refuse to take in more cats. This means that there are strays I could help but I am not helping. There are more cats who do not receive my help than cats who do receive my help. This is still true even if I donate money and food to the animal shelter.

We live in an imperfect world in imperfect times. I am not helping all of the animals; I am trying to help some of them. And I seek to avoid bringing harm to the ones who share this planet with me. I frequently think of the challenges we face in this life, on this planet, like this: it is a good news-bad news situation. The good news is we can donate our time and resources to any number of good causes. The bad news is that there are so many sentient beings that need our help.

> As you consider your life and your relationship with your pets and with the other animals around you, what will you do to follow the middle way? You might adopt more than two stray creatures, but you will not be able to adopt all of them.

> You live with more freedom and power than your furry, feathered, or scaly friends. In what way will you integrate the teachings about animals, the reality of this world, and your Buddhist practice?

The Buddha also lived in an imperfect world. He was against animal sacrifice and the harming of animals, but he lived among people who ate animal flesh, and he himself ate animal flesh. In his cosmology, animals have a place, and they are not as fortunate as humans. Their lives are shorter and more traumatic. They still have admirable qualities and can be examples to help us learn and grow. Despite their unfortunate rebirth and their difficult lives, we are to do our best to treat them with kindness and compassion. But we are human, and we will fall short. Our behavior and our intentions toward animals and others shape our karma, and our karma determines our rebirths and our ultimate freedom from suffering.

End Notes

[1] "Talk by Reiko Ohnuma at Stanford University - YouTube."

[2] James P. Mcdermott, "Animals and Humans in Early Buddhism," *Indo-Iranian Journal* 32, no. 4 (1989): 269–80.

[3] Mcdermott.

[4] Mcdermott.

[5] Ann Heirman, "How to Deal with Dangerous and Annoying Animals: A Vinaya Perspective," *Religions* 10, no. 2 (February 2019): 113, https://doi.org/10.3390/rel10020113.

[6] "The Many Ways Animals Teach Us Love, Compassion and Empathy - Animal Bonds," June 4, 2022, https://animal-bonds.com/the-many-ways-animals-teach-us-love-compassion-and-empathy/.

[7] Florin Deleanu, "Buddhist 'Ethology' in the Pāli Canon: Between Symbol and Observation," *The Eastern Buddhist* 32, no. 2 (2000): 79–127.

[8] Deleanu.

[9] Deleanu.

[10] Deleanu., page 114.

[11] Mcdermott, "Animals and Humans in Early Buddhism."

Chapter 5

Animals in Other Buddhist Cultures

In learning some of the Jātaka tales and the *suttas,* we are able to construct the beliefs and attitudes surrounding animals during the time of the Buddha. We have looked at how some of us treasure our animals and hold them in high esteem and at the evolution of our human-animal relationships. Now, let's take an opportunity to gain an understanding of how animals other Buddhist cultures view animals.

A major factor in the successful spread of Buddhism was that people could embrace Buddhist teachings without rejecting any of their preexisting beliefs. After the Buddha's death in the sixth to fourth century BCE, Buddhism began its journey of dissemination, facilitated by the dedicated efforts of its followers, who memorized and continued to spread the Buddha's teachings throughout India. Many of those who took up the practices and beliefs taught by the Buddha and his disciples were merchants. Engaging in commerce meant trade, and trade meant travel. Goods, spices, and ideas flowed along the trade routes. Buddhist monks traveled across the seas and along the land routes. Not all ideas take hold. But Buddhism did.

From a very general perspective, Buddhists do not seek to convert. When Buddhist monks journeyed to other lands, rarely did they demand that the people of those lands abandon their existing religions. And the result is that in addition to having three large divisions of Buddhism (Theravāda, Mahāyāna, and Vajrayana), the three schools practice Buddhism in different ways. This diversity in Buddhist practice has contributed to its enduring appeal across different cultures.

As a general rule, across all the schools and many ways of being Buddhist, animals are sentient beings and should be treated respectfully. Different cultures have encounters with different animal species and have an affinity for these species. While this book primarily provides a Western perspective, it's invaluable to explore the roles played by animals in other cultures where Buddhism thrives. The story of *The Journey to the West* is an excellent place to start.

The Journey to the West

In the sixteenth century, during the Tang Dynasty in China, the captivating tale known as *The Journey to the West* emerged. This timeless story revolves around the epic travels of Xuanzang, a courageous monk from the seventh century who boldly defied Emperor Taizong's travel restrictions to embark on a perilous journey in search of sacred Buddhist scriptures in what was then considered the West—India. Xuanzang's journey was long, arduous, and treacherous. He traversed northwest China to eventually cross what we now call Kyrgyzstan, Uzbekistan, Afghanistan, and northern Pakistan. Xuanzang traveled in India for thirteen years and although he had defied the wishes of the emperor, he returned to a hero's welcome. [1]

Xuanzang did not travel alone. He acquired four disciples who served and protected him. The first was Sun Wukong, the Monkey King. He began his life as a regular monkey, but after studying with a Taoist sage, he mastered the ability to fly and shapeshift, and he became immortal. What he did not do was learn to overcome his impatience and ego. He was enraged when he was excluded from a dinner party for the gods. He engaged in combat with the other gods and was on the verge of winning when the Jade Emperor called to the Buddha for assistance. The Buddha complied, and the Monkey King was buried at the bottom of a pile of rocks under a mountain. There he remained for five hundred years, until Xuanzang agreed to free him in exchange for his services as a bodyguard. [2]

Throughout the epic's one hundred chapters, Sun Wukong confronted a series of trials, many of which were posed by the Buddha himself. He was aided by companions such as Zhu Wuneng (the pig) and Sha Wujing (the river ogre), as well as the White Dragon Horse, as they battled demons, animal spirits, and other supernatural entities. [3]

Because he is an interesting character, the Monkey King became the breakout star of *The Journey to the West*. He is a trickster hero. If you recall, monkeys (and especially the Monkey King) also play important roles in some of the Jātaka tales. The Monkey King character may have been imported from Indian mythology. In the ancient Indian epic *Ramayana*, composed in the fourth century BCE, a monkey god named Hanuman played a crucial role in rescuing Sita from the demon king Ravana. This suggests a historical connection between Indian and Chinese mythologies, further enriching the tale's cultural depth.[4] The fact that Buddhism arrived in China by way of monks from India gives credence to this connection.

This ancient Chinese tale continues to resonate today, serving as a wellspring of inspiration for art, theater, movies, and television shows. As evidence of its enduring influence, Disney's 2023 release, *American Born Chinese*, draws heavily from the storyline of *The Journey to the West* and the 2006 novel *American Born Chinese*. It transports the narrative to modern Southern California, blending the challenges of growing up as an American-born child of Chinese immigrants with the quest for missing scrolls and a captivating Monkey King who can seamlessly shift between man and monkey. Also making an appearance is Guanyin, the *bodhisattva* of compassion.

In his article, "Is the Monkey King the world's most popular superhero?" James Trapp posits that "In many ways, the Monkey King is the archetype of the folk hero, or in modern terms, the superhero. There is no single Western equivalent of the Monkey King—perhaps a combination of Robin Hood, Hell Boy, and Shakespeare's Puck."[5] Trapp reminds us:

> Sun Wukong can change his shape at will and shrink his magic staff to the size of a needle, so he can keep it behind his ear. The martial arts elements of the story combine a sense of discipline and application with the sort of heroic skill that made films like

Crouching Tiger, Hidden Dragon such a success and have been a gift to film-makers over the years.

Despite his superpowers, at the heart of the Monkey King's appeal is his human fallibility—he is greedy, selfish, and prone to sudden changes of mood and outbursts of exceptional violence. He defies divine authority, laughs at attempts to be controlled, and leaves chaos in his wake. But we know that there is fundamental good within him.[6]

In *The Journey to the West* and the other tales that it has inspired, we can see the integration of Buddhism and other Chinese traditions with a respect for animals. It is also another example of how animals and stories about them can guide us on our own journey. The monk Xuanzang is dependent on the Monkey King. He cannot find the Buddhist scrolls and fulfill his destiny without the assistance of Sun Wukong. Defending the monk and accompanying him on his journey provides the Monkey King with the emotional and spiritual growth that he needs to gain his own salvation.

Rats in Bhutan

Pizza Rat was a popular internet meme that depicted a rat carrying a slice of pizza down the stairs into the New York City subway. This rat had scored an amazing meal. You probably do not wish to be reborn as a rat, but if you are, consider emulating Pizza Rat. Or seek to be reborn in Bhutan.

I once read a book about a woman who spent time teaching elementary school children in Bhutan. Her transition from life in the United States was difficult. She was subject to altitude sickness, culture shock, and cramped quarters with dirt floors and rats. She did not want to share her living quarters with rats. She woke up at night and heard them scurrying around her small room. Being part of a rat transportation network freaked her out, so she asked a local for advice on what to do to get rid of the rats. But she was met with silence. She thought that perhaps her question was not understood, so she brought it to her classroom.

Her young Buddhist students understood the question but were horrified at any solution that involved killing the rats. They told her that if she killed a rat, she would return as a rat in her next life, and if she killed another rat, she would return as a rat in the life after that one. The children felt very confident about this. Some of her students told her that they had relatives who had returned as rats. Now, she did not believe that someone had an uncle or a cousin who returned as a rat, but she got the point: no killing of rats or other living creatures.

Remember the *Vinaya*—the rules created by the Buddha so that he and his monks could live together harmoniously? Ordained Buddhist monks and nuns must follow these codes. There are rules about how to wear their robes, how and when to eat, the taking of medicine, how and where to sleep, and many other issues. At a high level, there is a Theravāda version, a Mahāyāna (or Chinese) version, and a Vajrayana version:

- The Theravāda version has 227 rules for monks and 311 for nuns.
- The Mahāyāna version has 253 rules for the monks and 348 for nuns.

- The Vajrayana versions has 253 rules for the monks and 364 for nuns.[7]

Why are there more rules for nuns? The answer depends on your perspective. These rules might be considered as a form of protection for unmarried women living without a family, or they might be considered misogyny in the form of women taking the blame for the bad behavior of their male counterparts.

Living in a monastic community at the time of the Buddha meant sharing your space with rats and other pests, which caused damage to blankets and food stores. For this reason, each version of the *Vinaya* discusses them, with rules to circumvent the damage they cause. The rules state not to store excess food, not just because it represents a form of wealth that monastics are not to exhibit, but also because it will attract rats and other pests. Meditation mats are to be shaken so as to dislodge anything that will attract rats. In the Theravāda *Vinaya,* a robe that has been chewed on by a rat is considered unclean and cannot be worn but may be torn apart and used as rags.

Because killing a sentient being is prohibited, the guidelines teach how people can protect themselves and their belongings from rats. But to purposefully kill one is a *pācittika* offense, meaning that it requires confession, followed by some type of penance. The guidelines are all about making it less likely that rats will plague you by making your space less attractive to them while at the same time doing them no harm and acknowledging that rats have a right to food and shelter.[8]

Circling back to the school children in Bhutan, they have the right idea—not that killing a rat will make you return as a rat but that killing a rat is undesirable. We should seek to avoid attracting rats, and we should make it difficult for them to access our necessities, but at the same time, we should view them with compassion. Even creatures that we consider to be dirty, undesirable, and annoying are trying to minimize their own suffering.

On Symbolism

With the Jātaka tales, we saw the importance of animals in teaching about the past lives of the Buddha and demonstrating behaviors that either help us move forward or hold us back. The *suttas* include animal similes and metaphors. Now, we will look at some specific instances where animals provide symbolism in certain Buddhist countries or locations but not necessarily all. For example, across many cultures and many Buddhist traditions, the elephant denotes wisdom and strength. But in the West, we may or may not recognize the elephant as a connection to Buddhism. You might connect the elephant to the circus or the zoo instead.

Dogs

In the story of Kukkuripa, enlightenment arrives in the form of a dog. Kukkuripa has ascended to the heavens but misses his dog. He wants to return to his dog but is convinced over and over again not to leave.

> As he gazed down from the heavens, he saw his beloved pet had become thin and sorrowful. It was then that he determined to come back to the cave. When both master and pup were reunited, joy filled their hearts as seemingly out of nowhere a

dakini appeared in place of the dog after being scratched by her master's hand! [9]

A dakini is recognized in Vajrayana Buddhism as a female messenger of wisdom. This story is well recognized in Vajrayana Buddhism, which is associated with Tibet. In Sri Lankan Buddhism, a dog would be an unlikely symbol of enlightenment.

Deer

Vajrayana deities are represented by animal counterparts, such as bears, boars, or deer. Begtse, known as the Goddess of Life, proudly rides atop a bear. Similarly, the boar is a fierce companion to another goddess. The deer is a reminder that the Buddha's first discourse occurred in a deer park. [10]

The deer is similarly well regarded in Japan, where in addition to symbolizing the first teachings of the Buddha, the deer represents peace and harmony. Nara Park in Japan combines World Heritage temples and reverence for deer. Todaiji Daibutsu temple was completed around 752 CE during the Nara Period. The Daibutsu (Great Buddha) is Japan's largest at fifteen meters high and was commissioned by Emperor Shomu to bring peace in the midst of the death of his infant son, a smallpox epidemic, and an attempted coup. [11]

Almost 1200 wild deer roam Nara Park. Legend has it that a white deer carried a god from Ibaraki, in northern Japan, down to Kasugataisha Shrine (a Shinto shrine), in a time when deer were considered sacred. Until

1637, killing a deer was punishable by death. Though no longer considered sacred, they are still protected. [12]

Nāgas

A *nāga* may be a snake, or it may look more like a dragon. *Nāgas* started out in Indian Buddhism as water spirits. Initially they looked like giant cobras, or they were portrayed as half-human and half snake. They were protectors of the Buddha and the Dharma. Legend has it that a *nāga* king kept the Buddha dry by coiling around him and turning his hood into an umbrella. Statues depicting this story are popular in parts of Southeast Asia.

In China, *nāgas* are commonly known as dragons. In some Buddhist countries, people make offerings to *nāgas* in order to solicit abundant crops, health, and fertility. A *nāga* will protect those who protect nature but breathe toxic air on polluters. [13] What an important reminder of our responsibility to the environment and to our planet.

Horses

The horse represents energy and effort, specifically in practicing the Dharma. Horses are loyal and swift, based on Kanthaka, the Buddha's own horse who helped him escape his father's palace and started him on his journey toward enlightenment. The neigh of the horse is symbolic of the Buddha's voice to awaken the sleepy mind to practice the Dharma. It also represents the prana, or breath, that is essential for our existence. Vajrayana has a mythical "Wind-Horse" that has the speed of the wind and the strength of the horse in order to guide the mind toward liberation. [14]

Lions

Because he bravely went against the wishes of his father and defied his clan, the Buddha has been called the "Lion of the Sakyas." He went off to seek enlightenment instead of staying home and becoming a leader. His voice is the Lion's Roar, proclaiming the Dharma. Lions are protectors of the teaching. You will see lions flanking the entrance to Buddhist temples. The lion is also the symbol of Sri Lanka. [15]

The Phoenix

The phoenix appears in times of peace and prosperity. Having risen from the ashes, the phoenix can also represent enlightenment. The ashes come from the death of ego. Chinese and Japanese culture used the phoenix (yin) and the dragon (yang) as the emblems for the emperor and the empress, as they symbolize a perfect marriage. In Confucianism, the phoenix displays the values of loyalty, honesty, decorum, and justice. In Chinese mythology, the phoenix is also one of the four spiritual creatures that guard the four directions and seasons: dragons, tigers, unicorns, and phoenix. [16]

The Lunar New Year

What year is it? I don't mean in the traditional Western chronological sense. I mean is it the year of the Rabbit, or the Dragon? What year were you born? Again, I am looking for your astrological animal. When you observe the Lunar New Year, you will know that you are welcoming the year of the Dragon or one of the other animal signs (twelve in total). This is a combination of astrology and Buddhism. In some American Chinese restaurants the placemats have depictions of the signs and the years in which they repeat. Additionally, the signs are modified by five elements: wood, fire, water, earth, and gold. These combinations of animal signs and elements are believed to shape your traits and, to some extent, your destiny.

From a Theravāda perspective, there is no evidence of the Buddha actually teaching this form of astrology, but there is a story that helps to fit this system into Buddhism. Once upon a time, the Buddha summoned all the beasts of creation before him with the promise of a gift for those who obeyed. Only twelve animals answered his call. As a reward, the Buddha named a year after each of his guests in the order of their arrival. And so the years are rat, ox, tiger, rabbit, dragon, snake, horse, goat, monkey, rooster, dog, and pig. The ox was actually the first to arrive, but the rat hitched a ride on the ox, hiding in his ear. And then just as the ox walked up, the rat jumped out of his ear and arrived just in front of him. [17] Because, you know, rats.

Going to the Dogs

To be a pug in ancient China! Why? Because you were treasured by the royalty. In fact, you were royalty. You may have had your own servants to attend to you. And for at least one of the emperors, his female pugs were considered to be just as valuable as his wives. If you stole a royal pug, you could expect to be sentenced to death.[18]

Pugs once kept Buddhist monks company in Tibetan monasteries and served as companion dogs for the wealthy. It is possible that they were first given as gifts to the monks by wealthy patrons. [19]

In his book Dharma Dogs: *Can Animals Understand the Dharma? Textual and Ethnographic Considerations,* James Stewart recounts a different story from Sri Lanka:

> A small, decrepit looking dog was staggering around the outer enclosure of the *stūpa*. As if from nowhere a lay temple attendant (*aebithyā*) appeared with a large stick to shoo the dog out of the enclosure. Having repeatedly struck the creature with the stick the dog quickly departed. [20]

Stewart attributes this behavior to the low status of dogs in Sri Lanka's cultural hierarchy. They are often considered impure and wretched creatures due to past misdeeds. Calling someone a dog is a grave insult in the Sinhala language. The attendant's swift action stemmed from the belief that the dog's presence polluted the sacred space near the *stupa*. [21]

While Stewart's reasoning for the temple attendant's behavior may be valid to some extent, it's essential not to generalize this treatment to all dogs in Sri Lankan temples. The teachings might remind us to treat all sentient beings with respect, but most of us are unenlightened humans and subject to our own cultural beliefs and emotions.

What we find here is how an animal might have an elevated status in one culture but not in another. The Vajrayana story of Kukkuripa features a well-respected, well-loved dog helping his master find enlightenment. Here, we have the presence of a dog interpreted as an insult. We are all subject to our cultural norms and belief systems.

While visiting Thailand several years ago, I observed that many temples had an abundance of stray cats and dogs living happily on their grounds. I learned that when people could not afford to feed their pets, they would drop them off at the temples. There, the animals would find a safe haven, as the monks would not harm them. In fact, at one temple, where we spent time on a brief retreat, I became fearful of the stray dogs. During the day, they wandered independently or slept in the shade. They seemed like sweet, carefree dogs living their best lives. After sunset, they formed a pack, and they became different dogs. Now, they took on the characteristics and behaviors of feral dogs. They were boisterous, territorial, and on the hunt. The caretakers warned me not to go out on my own. One of the caretakers would escort anyone who needed it from the meditation hall to the sleeping hall. Using a broom, he would gently keep the pack of dogs at bay.

Even in Buddhist countries, people are still simply people. And they are subject to their own challenges with dogs and their own cultural beliefs about dogs. A dog can be a royal pet, a royal pain, or something in between.

Cross-Cultural Connections

Varunthip Manthin loved her little dog Fou Fou with all her heart. When Fou Fou was hit by a car, Varunthip's heart was broken. She struggled to bid farewell to Fou Fou. It was easy to decide to hold a funeral on a scale of what she would have held for her own human child. Fou Fou was placed in a fuchsia-pink coffin and received funeral rites from a Buddhist monk.

These services were traditionally only held for humans. In response to the demand of their practitioners, monks now provide cremations and pet funerals as well, with the aim of securing a better rebirth for beloved pets. [23]

To meet the growing demand for pet funerals, monks like Theerawat Saehan have stepped forward to organize these services. They now oversee as many as three hundred such ceremonies every month. The most lavish may have been for a well-loved golden retriever, with sixty monks in attendance, eighty guests, a custom-made coffin, and a motorcade. [24]

Theerawat recalls receiving donations to pay for the funeral of one particular dog. This dog was a stray—street dog who frequented the local vegetable market. None of the vendors were wealthy, but many of them came together and donated small coins and bills to help pay for the funeral of this dog. Of the many pet funerals he officiated, Theerawat found this one to be the most touching. It was as if the street vendors were taking care of one of their own.[25]

Venerable Lungrik Gyaltsen, a Tibetan Buddhist monk in Southern California, went to Los Angeles airport to bless twenty dogs who had been rescued from meat markets in China. In addition to blessing the dogs, he set the intention for the facility providing temporary housing to the dogs to have protection and prosperity. [26]

Venerable Lungrik Gyaltsen stated, "We believe all living things have the same potential." He added, "Dog blessings, cat blessings—we've toured many states [in India], and we've blessed many people's pets. We bless for a healthy life for all sentient beings, not just humans." [27] And maybe these blessings will help them burn off some of their difficult karma and make it easier for them to be reborn in the human realm.

This special blessing of the dogs included sixteen golden retrievers, two corgis, one poodle, and one malamute and marked the official opening of Rue's Kennels, a part of China Rescue Dogs. The kennel is USDA and Border Patrol-governed. The CDC permits only facilities with those qualifications to receive rescue dogs from China, a high-risk rabies country. At the time of writing, China Rescue Dogs have saved over two thousand dogs from meat markets and breeding farms. [28]

Rue's and China Rescue Dogs exist due to the compassionate efforts of Jill Stewart. Jill's inspiration was a dog named Meeso, a disabled golden retriever she met in Shanghai in 2019. Meeso had been dumped on the streets, and a local Buddhist monastery adopted him. "No one had wanted this dog, and the monks blessed him," Stewart said. "I went to the Long Beach monastery to tell them my story and why it was so special to me to have a blessing." When she opened Rue's Kennels, the monks blessed it. In this way, Steward felt that what they had in Shanghai carried over to Los Angeles. As for Meeso, Jill felt a connection to him and brought him home. Meeso now lives in Southern California with Jill Stewart and her daughter. [29]

This convergence of Buddhism, human empathy, and our deep affection for animals showcases how they collectively guide us along the path to alleviate suffering. It is an example of using our elevated position to act as compassionate guardians for creatures who are less powerful.

> What legends and stories about animals did you grow up with? In what ways have these stories shaped your beliefs and attitudes? For example, you may have grown up being afraid of black cats or seeing a lady bug as a sign of good luck.

We do not all have *nāgas* or monkey kings. But we do learn from living with animals. In Buddhist cultures, stories about animals teach us how to behave, and the way we treat the animals around us defines who we are and where we are on our own spiritual journey. The further we travel, the more deeply we bond with our furry, feathered, and scaly friends. Yet these bonds are subject to impermanence. There will be a time when you must say goodbye.

End Notes

[1] "*Journey to the West*," in *Wikipedia*, July 29, 2023, https://en.wikipedia.org/w/index.php?title=Journey_to_the_West&oldid=1167716214.

[2] "How China's Monkey King Changed Western Literature," *Big Think* (blog), September 20, 2021, https://bigthink.com/culture-religion/monkey-king-literature/.

[3] "*Journey to the West*."

[4] "Is the Monkey King the World's Most Popular Superhero? | British Council," accessed August 6, 2023, https://www.britishcouncil.org/voices-magazine/monkey-king-worlds-most-popular-superhero.

[5] "Is the Monkey King the World's Most Popular Superhero?"

[6] "Is the Monkey King the World's Most Popular Superhero?"

[7] "The Bhikkhus' Rules: A Guide for Laypeople," accessed February 2, 2016, http://www.accesstoinsight.org/lib/authors/ariyesako/layguide.html.

[8] Ann Heirman, "What about Rats? Buddhist Disciplinary Guidelines on Rats: Daoxuan's Vinaya Commentaries," *Religions* 12, no. 7 (July 2021): 508, https://doi.org/10.3390/rel12070508.

[9] "Kukkuripa's Dog and the Sacred Animals in Buddhism — Power Animals of Enlightened Deities and Their Meaning - Buddha Weekly: Buddhist Practices, Mindfulness, Meditation," February 6, 2023, https://buddhaweekly.com/kukkuripas-dog-and-the-sacred-animals-in-buddhism-power-animals-of-enlightened-deities-and-their-meaning/.

[10] "Kukkuripa's Dog and the Sacred Animals in Buddhism — Power Animals of Enlightened Deities and Their Meaning - Buddha Weekly."

[11] "Todaiji Temple," Official Nara Travel Guide, accessed August 6, 2023, https://www.visitnara.jp/venues/A00485/.

[12] "Todaiji Temple."

[13] "Buddhist Symbols | Animals & Mythical Creatures: Dragon, Lion," accessed August 6, 2023, http://www.buddhistsymbols.org/animals.html.

[14] "Buddhist Symbols | Animals & Mythical Creatures: Dragon, Lion."

[15] "Buddhist Symbols | Animals & Mythical Creatures: Dragon, Lion."

[16] "Buddhist Symbols | Animals & Mythical Creatures: Dragon, Lion."

[17] S. Emerson Moffat et al., "Buddha Throws a Party," accessed August 6, 2023, https://www.austinchronicle.com/arts/2021-02-12/buddha-throws-a-party/.

[18] Denise Decker, "Chinese Pugs: History, Art, And More! | Kooky Pugs," December 19, 2020, https://kookypugs.com/chinese-pugs-history-art-and-more/.

[19] Denise Flaim Published: Apr 29, 2021 | 3 Minutes Updated: Aug 27, and 2021, "Pug History: Origins of the Ancient, Wrinkly Companion Dog," American Kennel Club,

accessed August 6, 2023, https://www.akc.org/expert-advice/dog-breeds/pug-history-ancient-companion-origins/.

[20] Stewart, "Dharma Dogs: Can Animals Understand the Dharma? Textual and Ethnographic Considerations."

[21] Stewart.

[22] Hannah Ellis-Petersen, "'A Ticket to the next Life': The Lavish Buddhist Dog Funerals of Bangkok," *The Guardian*, May 24, 2018, sec. Cities, https://www.theguardian.com/cities/2018/may/24/ticket-next-life-buddhist-dog-funerals-bangkok.

[23] "Buddhist Funeral Rites for Pets Gain Popularity in Thailand | Buddhistdoor," accessed August 6, 2023, https://www2.buddhistdoor.net/news/buddhist-funeral-rites-for-pets-gain-popularity-in-thailand#:~:text=In%20the%20Buddhist%20kingdom%20of%20Thailand%2C%20cremations%20for,reincarnating%20as%20higher%20beings%20in%20their%20next%20life.

[24] Ellis-Petersen, "'A Ticket to the next Life.'"

[25] Ellis-Petersen.

[26] Kate Karp, "Help Clear the Shelters before the 4th," *Long Beach Post* (blog), June 23, 2023, https://lbpost.com/newsletter/help-clear-the-shelters-before-the-4th/.

[27] Karp.

[28] Karp.

[29] Karp.

Chapter 6

Love Them and Let Them Go

The inspiration behind this entire book stems from our attachment to our pets and the grief we feel when our pets die. For some of us, the sadness that we feel when an animal friend dies can be just as painful and intense as when a person dies. But while the depth of our feelings may be similar to what we feel when we lose others, some of our approaches to working with those feelings might differ.

When people die, we have rituals and traditions to guide us through the process of continuing our lives. Most of them are designed to help those who have been left behind. Family and friends gather and sit with the survivors. Neighbors bring food. Our cultures, regions, religions, and communities offer guidelines regarding burial or cremation, who officiates, and when they must occur. There are informal or perhaps even formal rules around what color to wear. In the West, it is traditional to wear black. Others wear white, as is customary in Cambodian culture. If your family follows Thai traditions, the family wears black, and if there is a widow, she wears purple. Or you might all wear tropical prints because the deceased loved Hawaii. You might meet on the beach and paddle out into the water and release flowers. Maybe you hold a New Orleans-style jazz funeral. There are so many different ways in which we mourn our loss, celebrate a life, or both. I do not think that these rituals magically erase the grief, but they help. They bring us together and provide a sense of community. But what about when a pet has died? I think we are still figuring this out.

Cemeteries and Burials

In 1881, the back garden of Victoria Lodge in the Hyde Park section of London became an informal burial ground for pets. First, Cherry, a Maltese terrier, was buried, and then others brought pets to bury. All of this is due to the kindness of Mr. Winbridge, the park gatekeeper. Winbridge agreed to the burials and set aside land in the garden for them. In doing so, he started England's first pet cemetery. Paris established its first official pet cemetery in 1899, but the Cimetière des Chiens (Cemetery of Dogs) was not created to ease people's grief; it was founded to stop people from throwing their dead dogs into the River Seine. [1]

Now pet cemeteries serve practical, financial, and emotional needs. In Barcelona, the city council decided to create Spain's first public pet cemetery, with the idea that pet owners can have a burial similar to what would be held for a family member. And like the Cimetière des Chiens, this initiative is possibly not completely altruistic. At the time that I write this (spring 2023), it is estimated that there are 180,000 dogs in Barcelona and that 50 percent of residents own a pet. The city council estimates that the cemetery will perform about 7,000 ceremonies each year. That seems good for the people and good for the city budget. [2]

We treat our pets like family members, so it makes sense that some of us look at our own traditional practices as a reference point for how to treat our animals when they die. Cemeteries are a space where we keep the dead. A pet cemetery creates a place where we can memorialize our pets—a safe place to acknowledge the depth of your relationship with your pet and the depth of your grief. It is safe because the others who are there with you are doing the same thing. There is less judgement regarding how you choose to mourn.

Typically, a burial is part of a larger ceremony. There might be a religious service or a secular celebration of life. It is more than just placing a body in the ground. What might that look like for your pet? In the case of Susan Beasley's dog Cosmo, she knew what she wanted to do when he died. Susan, a Tibetan Buddhist, placed a sacred amulet on Cosmo's head and, with others, performed a traditional ceremony and feast offering. She left his body undisturbed for three days, just as she would have for a Tibetan Buddhist human. His final resting place was draped with white scarves, and pictures of him were surrounded with candles, incense, and rose petals. [3]

Prayers and Memorials

One day while out walking, I noticed a sign attached to the gate of one of my neighbors' houses. Within reach of the sign was a jar of dog treats and some dog toys. The sign had a picture of a dog leaping into the air, suspended, just moments before he caught a frisbee. I recognized that dog. The sign said that their beloved dog had died and that they knew that he would be happy if every dog who walked by took a treat from the treat jar or a toy from the box. In this way, this family was letting us all understand their sadness, and they were memorializing their beloved best friend. When it is time for you to say goodbye, you might do something similar, or you might elect to grieve privately.

If you would like to give your pet some help as they head for rebirth, you might use this Buddhist Prayer for Dying Animals:

> Oh Buddhas and Bodhisattvas of the ten directions and the three times, please protect and guide (your animal's name) on their journey. May they be free from fear and clinging to this life. May they have a happy and successful rebirth.
>
> *Om mani padme hum* (repeat this three times). [4]

This may help to bring you some peace, and you will know that your intentions are to help your pet move out of the animal realm.

At RainbowsBridge.com, you can find resources to help with your grief. You can create a virtual burial for your pet, selecting a location, perpetual time of year, and headstone. You can also place virtual toys and treats on this burial site. At the time of writing (spring 2023), this site was still active. It is definitely not a modern-looking website, but a quick check of memorials shows that people are still using this site to mark the passing of their pets and to write tributes and receive advice on how to help children process the death of a pet. Additionally, you can purchase urns, memorials, or marker stones, and even jewelry. Pet Heaven (https://petheaven.org/) offers you the ability to write an obituary for your pet. If you are not sure what to write or who to tell that your pet has died, then head over to Ever

Loved. (https://everloved.com/) Interestingly, Ever Loved is a site that is primarily for memorials to our human friends and family. Yet they have a section for pet memorials (https://everloved.com/pet-memorials/) in a list of available options and information toward the bottom of the home page.

Depending on where you live, you may be able to have your pet taxidermized or preserved. Honestly, I have bias here, and I mention it because it is a possibility, but I really encourage you to let the body of your pet go. In this way you can avoid clinging to the idea of your dead companion. Your friend is no longer in that earthly container, and it is not healthy for your emotional or spiritual well-being to keep the shell of their former existence as an ornament. I understand that your loss is significant, and seeing a version of your pet might seem helpful. But in the bigger context of your spiritual advancement, this is an opportunity to learn to accept the death of your beloved pet, to become more prepared for death, and to contemplate the breakup of the body. We are all meant to dissolve upon death. This is a lesson in impermanence.

Another way to remember your departed animal friend is through the creation of statues or portraits. You might have a nice statue created that you can place in your garden or in a location that you felt brought your furry friend comfort or joy. Recently, a friend lost a cat who had been by her side for many years. My friend was feeling this loss with every fiber of her being. Each morning, she would wake up, walk to the kitchen, and wait for her cat to rub against her legs, and then she would be overwhelmed with sadness as she remembered that her cat was dead.

About two weeks after the death of her cat, another friend surprised her with a beautiful painting of her cat. It was really nicely done and seemed to capture the essence of her cat during happier and healthier times. I know that this painting helped bring happy memories to our grieving friend.

The truth is you can create a pet portrait anytime. You probably already have many pictures of your favorite critter on your phone, and there are apps where you can upload a picture and have it turned into a portrait. Remember that 35 percent of us have more pictures of our pets than of our human family and friends. You do not have to wait until they die, but after they are gone, a nice picture, or a statue might bring you warm remembrances.

Cloning? Please Don't

A few years ago, a small group of us were having lunch together. One of the attendees began to tell us the story of how this extremely affluent woman had spent thousands of dollars to have her dog cloned. In this way, after her dog died, she had an exact replacement. This prompted some lively discussion. There were quite a few jokes and many questions. The woman who paid for the cloning process lived in the United States. The cloning took place in another country. Our consensus was that the dog had not really been cloned. A suitable lookalike had been found and presented to her as the clone of her deceased dog.

Many of us are going to outlive our pets. In fact, during our lifetime, we may see multiple pets go through the aging process. We love them, and each time a pet dies, we feel pain and sadness. For some this desire to alleviate that suffering might take the place of wanting to have a part of them continue. To avoid having to let go. This is an option for the very privileged. Today, a US-based company named ViaGen will clone your dog or cat for $50,000 or your horse for $85,000.[5]

Now, I realize that it is possible that the woman who had her dog cloned was not scammed. In 1996, when Dolly the sheep was born, we became aware of the possibility of animal cloning. Mice, rabbits, cattle, and cats were also successfully cloned. The first successful dog cloning was completed in 2005. Two dogs were cloned using the ear tissue from another dog. One died from pneumonia as a puppy. The other dog, named Snuppy, lived for ten years.[6]

The process for cloning, at least for dogs, involves many different dogs. First, cells (usually skin cells) are taken from your dog. Then unfertilized eggs are removed from a female dog, and the DNA from those eggs is replaced by the DNA from your dog. Those eggs are then placed in the uterus of a female dog. The success rate of the embryo becoming a viable puppy is at best about 20 percent. Sometimes the pregnant dog carries the embryo to term, but usually, at a certain point, the embryo is removed. In this process, many dogs have embryos implanted and have unsuccessful pregnancies, and some puppies are born with defects or die soon after birth. For one successful cloning, many dogs must be used as laboratory animals.[7]

When that successful cloning occurs, it is not really your same dog. This is an important distinction. A clone will look like the original, but it is not the original. Alexandra Horowitz, author of *Inside of a Dog: What Dogs See, Smell, and Know* and a researcher of canine cognition, reminds us that what you love about your dog—the dog's personality—is not in the genes of the cloned dog. She acknowledges that there are tendencies within each breed, so a clone will be similar in behavior, but what you really love about your dog's personality cannot be cloned.[8]

It is that companionship, that special bond, that you are clinging to, and it is the idea of being without that companion that you are trying to avoid. After all the time and money spent in the cloning process, and the suffering inflicted on other dogs, you will not have your exact dog returned to you.

If you really need some type of replica of your pet, perhaps the most humane and appealing approach is to have a plush version created—a high-quality lookalike stuffed animal (stuffed as in a toy, not as in taxidermy or freeze dried). This is not your pet or an actual animal. It is a cheerful reminder. You are in good shape as long as you understand that this plush toy is a way of commemorating your friend. Better yet, donate to an animal shelter. You can make the donation in honor of your deceased pet. You gave your special creature a happy and secure life. Now your donation can help do the same for those who are waiting for a forever home.

Consider keeping a few pictures around, and work with your grief and loss. When you are used to taking long walks with your dog, cuddling on the couch with your cat, or sharing your deepest thoughts and fears with your bird, their absence will create a void. There is nothing wrong with finding a way to keep happy memories alive.

Let Your Practice Inform Your Choice

When I was a child and our puppy died, I had no idea what happened to her after the fact. She disappeared, and I missed her. Now, the veterinarian provides cremation services. In 2001, I brought my beloved cat Biff in to be cremated, and they took his body and offered me condolences. In 2017 with Maple, and then in 2019 with Alex, they asked if I wanted to keep the ashes. In light of the fact that you can have a burial and a ceremony or even release the ashes, this makes sense. You might decide to keep the ashes, and if you do not bury them, keep them in an urn, or release them, you can have those ashes made into pottery or even jewelry. If you did not begin this chapter with an understanding of the options available to you, I think you understand them now. And there must be other ways to celebrate the life of your pet and mourn the loss of your pet, ways that go beyond what I have covered. These options provide a range of ways to commemorate the life of your pet and find solace in your Buddhist practice.

While conducting the research for this chapter, I encountered a story that makes my heart happy. And I hope it will do the same for you. Kevin Curry and his dog Mellow walked twice daily most days for approximately seven years. Mellow was a rescue dog who found his forever home with Kevin. In 2023, Kevin learned that Mellow had lymphoma. Mellow was dying. Many of the neighbors knew Mellow because he and Kevin walked, rain or shine. Kevin decided that Mellow needed a send-off. A final walk around the neighborhood. Kevin prepared a special letter and left it in mailboxes all along their usual walking route.

Curry wrote a letter on Mellow's behalf:

I will be marching around the neighborhood on Saturday, June 3 from 7-8PM and would love to say goodbye to you face-to-face if you are available, come out to pat me on the head or rub my belly and I will be forever grateful (I love people after all). [9]

On the day and time of the final walk, Kevin set out, expecting a small turnout of supportive neighbors. There were crowds of people. Children made signs; some people brought their dogs. Mellow had the best possible experience. He was a rescue dog who lived his best life and was loved by many. [10] Together Kevin and Mellow brought together an entire community. Many of the people who turned out did not even know them. But they knew the importance of the relationship between a man and his dog and the courage it took to take this one final walk.

We can hope that after Mellow died, friends and neighbors continued to check in on Kevin and remind him that, like his dog, he is loved. That is what we can do for our friends, colleagues, and family members after they lose a cherished pet. Kevin's act of kindness reminds us that even in our pets' final moments, we can create meaningful experiences that celebrate their lives and the love they shared.

This Is Personal

When someone you know loses their furry, feathered, or scaled companion, acknowledge their loss. When they are ready, share stories about what was so great about the pet. Spend time with them. Go for a walk with them, or maybe help out by bringing meals. You can also help them clean up after the pet or pack away toys and bedding. Everyone goes through this in their own way. While we might not understand someone's sadness, we know that there is sadness.

After your pet dies and you decide whether to have a burial, cremation, ceremony, or nothing, you will still be faced with your own grief. Please be sure that the approach you use to say goodbye is in the absolute best interest of your spiritual growth. This requires self-awareness and honesty on your part. Will keeping a picture, statue, ashes, or plush version of your pet allow you to fully express your grief and ultimately accept the fact that your sweet critter is gone? Your work now is to be with your grief.

Grief is a very personal process. In Buddhism, the practice of mindfulness and acceptance can provide valuable tools for navigating grief. Know that most of us are still going to feel grief. Do not judge yourself harshly because you struggle with sadness and loss. Buddhism does not necessarily stop the pain of grief. It helps us understand it, sit with it, and fully feel it.

When I interviewed several different Buddhist teachers for *Sitting with Death: Buddhist Insights to Help You Face Your Fears and Live a Peaceful Life*, I learned that even those who are advanced on the path work with sadness. Do not place unrealistic expectations on yourself. All Buddhists know death and loss. All of us encounter impermanence. Each time we do, it is different, and with different degrees of difficulty, running the gamut of emotions. And when we opt to live with animals with lifespans shorter than our own, we repeat this cycle multiple times. Do your best to prepare yourself. You can start by becoming comfortable with impermanence. Adopt a pet. Love your pet, and enjoy your time together. Do not forget that your time together is finite. It is the temporary nature of your relationship that can make it so sweet. Be mindful of the expectations you create around your life and relationship with your pet, and acknowledge where you have attachment.

Giving a loving and secure home to a feathered, furry, or scaly critter is a gift to each of you. You develop a meaningful relationship, and you have the ability to help your companion become closer to a better rebirth. In turn, during their lifetime, they can bring you much-needed support.

End Notes

[1] "What I Think about When I Say Goodbye to My Beloved Dying Pet | Aeon Essays," Aeon, accessed August 6, 2023, https://aeon.co/essays/what-i-think-about-when-i-say-goodbye-to-my-beloved-dying-pet.

[2] Mona Zahir, "Buddhism And Animal Ethics," Faunalytics, April 26, 2018, https://faunalytics.org/buddhism-animal-ethics/.

[3] Tami Simon, ed., *The Dharma of Dogs: Our Best Friends as Spiritual Teachers* (Boulder, CO: Sounds True, 2017)., page 85.

[4] Molly De Shong, "Lama Zopa on Caring for Your Animals - Lions Roar," September 15, 2008, https://www.lionsroar.com/lama-zopa-on-caring-for-animals/.

[5] "Pet Cloning Process, Clone Your Dog, Cat Cloning, Dog Cloning," *Viagen Pets* (blog), accessed August 6, 2023, https://www.viagenpets.com/product/initiate-cloning/.

[6] Smithsonian Magazine and Jacob Brogan, "The Real Reasons You Shouldn't Clone Your Dog," Smithsonian Magazine, accessed August 6, 2023, https://www.smithsonianmag.com/science-nature/why-cloning-your-dog-so-wrong-180968550/.

[7] Magazine and Brogan, "The Real Reasons You Shouldn't Clone Your Dog."

[8] Magazine and Brogan.

[9] "Man Takes Dying Dog for Final Walk around PA Neighborhood — and Neighbors Show out Big," accessed August 6, 2023, https://www.yahoo.com/news/man-takes-dying-dog-final-140738368.html.

[10] "Man Takes Dying Dog for Final Walk around PA Neighborhood — and Neighbors Show out Big."

Chapter 7

Animals to the Rescue

Many of us find solace and support in the companionship of our pets during life's toughest moments. We face challenges with our health, issues at work, breakups and death. Dr. Margaret Paul, an associate professor of psychiatry at the University of California, Davis, authored a study that found that having a pet changes our behavior, helping us to feel more connected to others. Part of the findings have to do with how pet ownership can help us move forward after the loss of a loved one. Of the one thousand people surveyed over the course of ten years, those who had a pet reported being self-sufficient and in good emotional health six months after the loss. Another related study found that having a pet is helpful during times of personal crisis. [1]

In a poignant episode of *After Life* on Netflix, we witness how a pet can provide a lifeline in moments of despair. We find Tony, a recent widower, sitting in his bathtub. It's full of water, and he holds a razor up to one of his wrists. Losing the love of his life to cancer has brought him to the lowest of lows. He questions why he should live, and he does not know how to go on without her. He looks like he is about to slash his wrists. All of a sudden, there is a soft whimper. He looks toward the open bathroom door, where his dog, Brandy, stands with an expectant look on her face. Tony says, "Are you, hungry, girl?" And with that, he puts the razor down, drains the tub, and follows his dog into the kitchen, thoughts of suicide behind him for now. The scene is beautifully expressive—one of many that show how our bonds with our furry family members help our mental health. And during the grieving process, most of us need help.

When my mother and my husband died within five days of one another, I felt as if I had been cut in half lengthwise. I was thrown completely off balance; nothing was quite working. There I sat in my house with my two cats. At that time, they were already twelve and thirteen years old. I thought that perhaps the Murphy's Law of death meant that at any moment, one or both of those cats would die. And then I really would be completely alone. Sometimes I would look at them and say, "Please don't die. Please don't die. Just stay for at least another year." That was silly because I already knew there was no bargaining with death. Fortunately, one lived three more years, and the other an impressive five additional years.

While cats do not always receive high marks for being caring or empathetic, my two definitely rallied around me. One of them was always right next to me. Sometimes I wondered if perhaps they had set up some type of agreed-upon schedule. One had mornings; the other had afternoons, and they both took evenings. At night when I was trying to sleep, one or both of them would curl up right next to me. Maybe it was because there was extra room in the bed, or maybe it was cold. But I knew that I was not alone.

In *After Life,* Tony makes a comment to Brandy that if she could open her own food tins, he would be dead. The healing power of having a pet to take care of cannot be overemphasized. While I never felt suicidal, certainly I experienced depression. Having two furry creatures depending on me for their care was a great way to help take me out of myself. For a few moments each day, my thoughts were directed toward their care. One of them had been especially close to my husband, Ed, and I worried about how she would handle his death. She became my "watch cat." It seemed like every time I turned around, there she was, keeping an eye on me.

I'm so glad that my two cats were part of my grief journey. Here are some of the benefits that our pets provide us while we navigate the loss of a loved one:

1. Taking care of your pet gives you a purpose—something to do beyond feeling sad or taking care of the business of death.

2. Some days you might not be ready for the company of other humans, but you do not want to be all alone.

3. When you come home, you are not coming back to an empty house. You have someone waiting for you on the other side of the door.

4. When you talk to yourself, you have a listener. And that makes a big difference. You find you are not just talking to yourself after all.

5. Your pet can be a link to your deceased loved one. If you shared a pet together, now that pet is part of a happy shared memory.

6. Pets (especially cats) are a good reminder that you are not the center of the universe.

7. Sometimes your pets do unpredictable things—dragging ribbons out of the closet, knocking over flowers, or jumping on your bladder to wake you up. All of these things are welcome distractions, and some make you smile or perhaps even help you laugh.

While our pets can be incredible sources of support, remember that seeking professional assistance is crucial if you ever find yourself in a dark place.

Pet Therapy

Pet therapy is beneficial for a wide range of people, not just those dealing with grief. There was a time when my mother-in-law resided in an assisted living facility. She was not thrilled about moving, but it did allow her to have the right amount of independence and the right amount of care. The nearby location allowed me to visit her a few days a week. And as I did, I began to learn the schedule. The activities coordinator worked to create an environment where each day residents could be as social or reclusive as they desired. There were residents who were very mobile, active, and talkative. One elderly man zipped around in his electric wheelchair. He was fast and furious. Emphasis on furious. He would come to events but seemed to be quite angry much of the time. And if you did not move out of his way, he might run you over.

On Friday afternoons, they had happy hour with music and dancing. On Sunday mornings, there was a visit from a church group, and on one Sunday afternoon each month, the dogs came to visit. Some of the residents had their own cat or small dog, but most did not. That monthly visit of friendly dogs was a popular event. Although I'm not certain of their name, I know that a local therapy dog organization brought the dogs. About four or five dogs came to visit, and anyone who wanted to interact with them came downstairs and sat in the lobby area.

One of my favorite interactions was between the man in the electric wheelchair and the dogs. The man was mostly nonverbal, although there were times when I saw him appear to have a tantrum and lash out at others. When the dogs were there, he seemed changed. He smiled from ear to ear, just happily petting one of the dogs.

Those dogs brought many smiles to all involved. Whether it was someone who really wanted to pet and cuddle a pup or someone like my mother-in-law who preferred to watch from a distance. During these visits I saw firsthand the value of the human-animal bond. The atmosphere was one of joy. And it seemed like the dogs were happy too. Not just because of the endless attention. They had an air of satisfaction, as if they knew that they were fulfilling their purpose.

Spending time with pets is helpful but not a complete remedy. Individuals who participated in surveys about the perks of having pets consistently agreed that pets are not a cure for mental health challenges. The consensus was that pets can play an important role and help prevent worsening of symptoms. Pets can help make life more enjoyable while symptoms are present. [2]

Pets can bring us joy and help us with our mental and emotional health. Specific benefits include:

- A chance to feel pleasure
- Increased motivation
- Reduced anxiety
- Decreased number of panic attacks
- More social connections

These benefits help reduce loneliness. Now, having a pet is not a complete solution, and it is not helpful to everyone. In March 2020, the *Journal of Affective Disorders* published findings regarding pet ownership and depression in older adults. Most of the results were primarily positive, yet sometimes pet ownership can increase negative feelings and emotional strain. [3]

Not everyone is suited for pet ownership. In fact, it can lead some people to feel more anxious. For some, having another life requiring care and feeding is more pressure. And a new pet owner can feel overwhelmed with the responsibility and uncertainty around how to take care of this creature. Moreover, in a study on cats and their impact on depression and anxiety, sometimes new cat owners did not feel better. The duties of training the cat, cleaning the litter box, taking the cat to the vet, and finding a pet sitter added to anxiety levels. [4] Before taking the leap into pet ownership, take the time to research and ask questions. Ensure that the choice is right for both you and the animal, and consider seeking guidance from experts in pet care.

Horses Can Help Us

Around 10,200 BCE, humans began interacting with wild horses, capturing and domesticating them. Horses played vital roles in labor, transportation, and even warfare, often fighting alongside soldiers. These interactions formed strong bonds between humans and domesticated horses. Today, horses are more commonly pets or therapy animals. [5]

Horses display emotions and are capable of making complex facial expressions. We recognize some of those expressions and emotions, and this makes it easier for us to relate to them. And they can understand us. For these and many other reasons, hippotherapy, or horse therapy, can help us with our mental, emotional, and physical well-being. Hippotherapy is not new, yet at the time of writing, there is not a lot of concrete data on its efficacy. [6]

In 1996, members of the Department of Psychology at Doshisha University, Karasuma-imadegawa, Kamigyo-ku, Kyoto, Japan, conducted a survey to learn more about the effect of companion animals on humans and vice versa. For their study, they worked with men and horses. The results showed that petting a horse has a calming effect. Specifically, it helps lower your heart rate. The study included three groups, each made up of six men. Group one had positive attitudes toward pets. Group two had negative attitudes toward pets. Group three were members of a horse-riding club. In all cases, after ninety seconds spent petting a horse, the human participants' heart rates decreased. As for the horses, initially their heart rates elevated, but then they decreased as the petting continued. Authors of the study concluded that this demonstrated that petting horses decreases tension and that there was an emotional interaction between the men and the horses. [7]

Horseback riding can help individuals recover from trauma due to its ability to encourage emotional development. Engaging with a horse fosters confidence as riders learn to guide the horse assertively and build trust. The bond between horse and rider deepens, allowing for enhanced nonverbal communication. This can improve patience, trust, and communication skills while increasing empathy and the ability to feel affection toward others. The rider learns they need to give directions decisively and assertively. The rider also begins to access nonverbal communications. You can give the horse verbal commands, but the horse does not talk back. At least not verbally. A horse responds with facial expressions, or with a toss of the head, and other movements. The bond that the rider develops with the horse can help you increase your empathy and ability to feel affection toward others. In short, a positive bond with a horse builds your patience, trust and communication skills. [8]

Horseback riding is also helpful for physical and occupational therapy. When used for physical therapy, the movement of the horse can mimic the movements that a human pelvis makes during walking. Different gaits help a therapist to understand sensory stimulation in a patient, and that helps to develop a treatment plan aimed at reaching specific healing goals. Horseback riding also helps with balance and posture. For occupational therapy, the movements of the horse help improve motor control, coordination, and focus. The benefit is that it stimulates multiple areas at the same time. Working with the horse requires seeing, hearing, and touching. It also requires the patient to be aware of their body in relationship to the horse. [9]

In his book *Animal Sutras: Animal Spirit Stories,* the late Stephen Levine tells the story of the Karmapa's Horse. In Vajrayāna Buddhism, the Karmapa is a consciously reborn lama and leader of a subbranch of one the four schools of Tibetan Buddhism. Stephen Levine, a well-respected teacher, author, and poet who helped to make the teachings of Theravāda Buddhism accessible in the West, was at a gathering to meet the Karmapa. This was an honor and also a privilege. Followers believed that the Karmapa's horse gave blessings by placing one of its hooves on an individual's head. Some people received a light touch, and occasionally a person got a pretty good whack. This was an intimidating prospect. If you received the light touch, you might hear a light hum of the chant *om mani padme hum*. Nobody wanted to get kicked in the head. Stephen received a blessing from the Karmapa but did not encounter his horse. But he did have his own experience of being one with a horse. He wrote about riding his own horse, Duster, and feeling a sense of oneness: "Surrendering in the saddle with your hair blowing back on the verge of impermanence is a little different than surrendering on your quiet mediation pillow. The mesa had

a lot to teach me, and Duster was one of my guru sisters on the journey."
10

Prison Programs

To live in prison is *dukkha,* or suffering. For four years, I participated in monthly visits to one of our California state prisons. This was volunteer work I did alongside my colleague Venerable De Hong as part of the Engaged Buddhist Alliance (https://engagedbuddhistalliance.org/). Our goal was to bring Buddhist meditation to the incarcerated in the hopes that they learned a helpful tool to ease their time and exit the cycle of recidivism. I learned that the actions that led to incarceration bring suffering to all parties. I heard stories with similar themes; many of our incarcerated have come from a cycle of abuse, abandonment, and addiction (this does not justify the crimes they have committed). I worked with a relatively small group of men who attended our program in order to learn Buddhist meditation to help them make changes in their lives. Some came just to earn credits to help them qualify for release, but most were looking for a way toward personal growth and to step away from the patterns of behavior that led to their incarceration.

According to the Vera Institute of Justice, the United States is home to 4 percent of the world's population, and 16 percent of the total number of incarcerated individuals in the world. [11] The Vera Institute of Justice is a group of researchers, activists, and advocates, all working toward reducing mass incarceration and providing just, anti-racist solutions for the people in the justice and immigration systems. In the United States, we have an opportunity to find ways to rehabilitate our incarcerated population. They are suffering, and some, upon release, will return to committing crimes, which means more suffering for them and their friends, family, and community. Education is helpful. Consistently, the data on education and recidivism reflects that the higher the level of education received while incarcerated, the less likely an individual is to return, and the more successful that individual will be with their job search. Along with traditional education, it is useful for incarcerated individuals to attend the following:

- Communication skills courses
- Conflict resolution courses
- Forgiveness programs
- Trade school

The Buddhist meditation classes held by the Engaged Buddhist Alliance are helpful to some. Others might prefer a more traditional religious service. It is definitely not a one-size-fits-all scenario. And within this mix of rehabilitation programs, sometimes the opportunity to work with dogs or cats can make a difference. This is where programs such as New Leash on Life bring value.

Philadelphia-based New Leash on Life (https://newleashonlife.org/about-us/) states that they give humans and canines a second chance. They rescue dogs at risk of being euthanized from shelters and place them in a training program to teach them behaviors that will make them adoptable. Many of the dogs were at risk because they would not be able to live successfully with humans. Incarcerated individuals who qualify for New Leash on Life learn how to care for the dogs. After training, the dogs may become available for adoption by the general public or by an individual after they are released from prison. Prison officials select human program participants, but those who have committed crimes such as animal abuse, child abuse, sexual abuse, or arson are not qualified to participate. [12]

In November 2019, Mia Trett was injured in a violent attack on campus at Saugus High School in Santa Clarita, California. Her doctor recommended a service dog to help with her recovery. That is where the Paws for Life program enters the story. Paws for Life (https://pawsforlifek9.org/paws-for-life-prison-program/) is a dog rescue organization, and one of their initiatives is a prison program. Paws for Life takes dogs from shelters and brings them to one of three California state prisons for training. In 2020, more than 185 incarcerated men took part in the training program. Mia's service dog, Brandy, trained at Los Angeles County Lancaster. Mia's wise observation was, "It's not like anyone wants to be in prison, but if you're going to be here, you might as well do something great—no matter who they are." [13]

Pawsitive Change is a prison program that takes dogs from high-kill shelters to qualified students in the California state prison population. Marley's Mutts, a dog rescue organization, oversees the program. The goal is to help prevent the euthanasia by turning the dogs into valued pets. The dogs and students live together for three months. The end result is that most of the students become skilled dog trainers, and most of the dogs become adoptable. This translates into human beings who are team-oriented and emotionally aware and who have heightened self-esteem and feel that they are able to add value to society. [14]

In these programs, the bond between humans and animals helps to reduce suffering for both parties. Dogs and humans who have a low probability of making valuable contributions to society become changed beings. Through their encounters, they heal some of the wounds and trauma that led them to act harmfully. When the end result is an adoptable dog, a trusted service dog, or a human who becomes a productive member of society, the benefits extend to the community at large.

Cat Videos Rule the Internet

You might not be dealing with grief or recovering from a traumatic injury, and you might not have access to horses. But for a quick fix to alleviate some mild symptoms of depression and anxiety, watch a cat video. "If you get a warm, fuzzy feeling after watching cute cat videos online, the effect may be more profound than you think." [15]

For her study published in *Computers in Human Behavior* in 2015, Jessica Gall Myrick surveyed almost 7,000 people about their viewing of cat videos and how it affected their moods. "Some people may think watching online cat videos isn't a serious enough topic for academic research, but the fact is that it's one of the most popular uses of the Internet today," Myrick said. "If we want to better understand the effects the Internet may have on us as individuals and on society, then researchers can't ignore Internet cats anymore." [16]

Myrick's study included self-proclaimed "cat people" and people who liked both dogs and cats. The participants felt more energetic and positive after watching cat-related online media. They reported a decrease in anxiety, annoyance, and sadness. Some watched the videos as a form of procrastination to avoiding working or studying. Procrastinators felt that the benefits derived from watching the cat videos outweighed any feelings of guilt. "Even if they are watching cat videos on YouTube to procrastinate or while they should be working, the emotional pay-off may actually help people take on tough tasks afterward," Myrick said. [17]

To be human is to experience suffering. We are constantly dealing with attachment and aversion. Right there with us are our furry, feathered, or scaly friends. They might provide assistance in our daily lives—for example, helping us to walk or to detect danger. We might benefit from petting them or holding them. Or perhaps knowing that there is another being sitting next to us is enough to ward off or decrease anxiety or depression. Interacting with your special critter can increase your ability to feel compassion for other beings. You know that you feel deeply when your pet suffers, and you seek to alleviate that suffering. When living with a pet brings you peace of mind, you are more likely to make gains in your spiritual practice. It is easier to wish goodwill to yourself and others when your mind is calm.

End Notes

[1] "Pets: Good Companions Or Not? – PatchPets," January 4, 2023, https://www.patchpets.com/pets-good-companions-or-not/.

[2] Roxanne D. Hawkins, Emma L. Hawkins, and Liesbeth Tip, "'I Can't Give Up When I Have Them to Care for': People's Experiences of Pets and Their Mental Health," *Anthrozoös* 34, no. 4 (July 4, 2021): 543–62, https://doi.org/10.1080/08927936.2021.1914434.

[3] Hawkins, Hawkins, and Tip.

[4] "You, Your Cat, and Anxiety or Depression," Psych Central, May 13, 2019, https://psychcentral.com/health/your-cat-depression-anxiety.

[5] "10 Things That Make Horse & Human Relationships So Unique | Agape," *Pet Urns & Pet Cremation Services | MD | VA | NC* (blog), October 17, 2019, https://agapepetservices.com/make-horse-human-relationships-unique/.

[6] "10 Things That Make Horse & Human Relationships So Unique | Agape."

[7] "10 Things That Make Horse & Human Relationships So Unique | Agape."

[8] "10 Things That Make Horse & Human Relationships So Unique | Agape."

[9] Tuba Tulay Koca and Hilmi Ataseven, "What Is Hippotherapy? The Indications and Effectiveness of Hippotherapy," *Northern Clinics of Istanbul* 2, no. 3 (January 15, 2016): 247–52, https://doi.org/10.14744/nci.2016.71601.

[10] Stephen Levine, *Animal Sutras: Animal Spirit Stories* (Rhinebeck, New York: Monkfish Book Publishing Company, 2019), 41–44.

[11] "Who We Are," Vera Institute of Justice, accessed August 6, 2023, https://www.vera.org/who-we-are.

[12] "ABOUT US - New Leash on Life," December 12, 2019, https://newleashonlife.org/about-us/, https://newleashonlife.org/about-us/.

[13] Don Chaddock editor Inside CDCR, "Saving Dogs, Helping People," Inside CDCR, March 4, 2020, https://www.cdcr.ca.gov/insidecdcr/2020/03/04/saving-dogs-helping-people/.

[14] "Pawsitive Change," Marleys Mutts, accessed August 6, 2023, https://www.marleysmutts.org/pawsitivechange.

[15] "Not-so-Guilty Pleasure: Viewing Cat Videos Boosts Energy, Positive Emotions," ScienceDaily, accessed August 6, 2023, https://www.sciencedaily.com/releases/2015/06/150616093357.htm.

[16] "Not-so-Guilty Pleasure."

[17] "Not-so-Guilty Pleasure."

Chapter 8

Your Responsibility

Jane Goodall once wisely said, "You cannot share your life with a dog and not know perfectly well that animals have personalities, minds, and feelings." This sentiment forms the cornerstone of our discussion on the profound connection between humans and their animal companions. Knowing that your dog, or cat, or bird has a specific way of being, feels hunger and pain, and enjoys companionship, how can you do anything less than to nourish and protect this creature? You have brought this special being into your world; now you must make sure that you are always considering their needs.

In Hawaiian, someone who lives with a pet is a *kahu*. If you live with a pet, you are the guardian or protector of a creature who is sacred and precious. This speaks to the responsibility we have to treat the animals around us with love and respect. To acknowledge that we all have an important role in this world. We are to behave as trusted caretakers of the planet and all its species.

While I've used the term "pet owner" for conventional purposes in this book, my hope is that you and I will collectively honor the preciousness of our pets and recognize that they rely on us to be their loving custodians. In the words of the late 25th Tulku Rinpoche, "For me, an animal is not something for me to keep. I do not think of them on the basis of what they will do for me. What I like to do is make sure that they are free from pain, mental anxiety, and disease and that they live in a healthy environment."[1] You know that you need to give your animal friends food, shelter, affection, and medical care. That is the minimum. But take a more expansive view. If they really are your friends, or your family, then you need to make them your priority.

PETS Act

With the rise of the interspecies family, many of us have improved the care we give our pets. That has extended to the evacuation of pets and service animals during and following a major disaster or emergency. This act was necessary after Hurricane Katrina devasted New Orleans in 2005, and half of the residents refused to evacuate without their pets.[2] Katrina was the costliest hurricane to hit the United States and one of the five deadliest hurricanes in terms of loss of human life.

Those who stayed with their pets suffered from food deprivation, dehydration, and sometimes death. Despite the harsh conditions, many people refused to accept help in the form of relocation unless it included their pets. Because responders were not allowed to assist with pets, many shelters would not accept animals, so people who went to shelters were typically faced with abandoning their pets. The results were grim: over one hundred thousand pets were left behind or set free, and seventy thousand of them died.[3]

We owed them so much more. The Pets Evacuation and Transportation Standards Act of 2006 took steps to ensure that pets and service animals are included in state and local emergency preparedness operational plans. The PETS act authorizes the Federal Emergency Management Agency (FEMA) to provide care, shelter, food, and evacuation assistance to households with service animals and pets:

> Pets Evacuation and Transportation Standards Act of 2006 - Amends the Robert T. Stafford Disaster Relief and Emergency Assistance Act to require the Director of the Federal Emergency Management Agency (FEMA) to ensure that state and local emergency preparedness operational plans address the needs of individuals with household pets and service animals prior to, during, and following a major disaster or emergency. Specifically, the PETS Act,
>
> Authorizes the Director to: (1) study and develop plans that take into account the needs of individuals with pets and service animals prior to, during, and following a major disaster or emergency; and (2) make financial contributions, on the basis of programs or projects approved by the Director, to the states and local authorities for animal emergency preparedness purposes, including the procurement, construction, leasing, or renovating of emergency shelter facilities and materials that will accommodate people with pets and service animals. [4]

The PETS act is a step in the right direction but is imperfect. Shortcomings include:

- It only includes dogs, cats, birds, rabbits, rodents, and turtles.

- If a local government has a ban against a certain type of dog—for example, pit bulls—then there is no requirement to include those animals as part of a rescue plan.

- There is confusion as to whether locations acting as emergency shelters must accept pets.

- It does not include horses or livestock. [5]

The impact of a hurricane on farm animals and livestock became painfully obvious in 2018, when Hurricane Florence made landfall in North Carolina. Three and a half million farm animals were left to face the storm and the flood waters that came with it. Many of these pigs, chickens, cows, and other animals were caged and did not have the opportunity to flee or to fend for themselves; they were trapped and at the mercy of the wind and water. Reports from that time indicate that the majority of them died.[6]

It is an ugly truth that animals are considered property and that farm animals are a business investment. They are covered under insurance policies that treat them as things that can be valued at a certain price and are reimbursable for a price. These are not life insurance policies.

None of this absolves us from our responsibility to care for them and to seek to alleviate their suffering. A legal classification of property does not reflect the true nature of things. The emergency care of three and a half million animals is mind boggling. I am not naïve enough to think that there is a quick and safe way to transport all of those animals. But we are fortunate to have state and federal agencies to assist us during times of crisis. The valuable support they provide is not a complete solution. We also need to take responsibility for our own well-being and for the well-being of the animals around us. For those of us with pets, that means having some type of carrying case or bag to transport them, as well as extra food and water and any prescriptions they may need.

As for the farm animals, the United States Humane Society offers tips on how to be disaster ready. These tips include high perches for poultry so that they can evade flood waters. Reinforce your house, barn, and other structures with hurricane straps. Use native and deep-rooted plants because they are less likely to become uprooted during a storm. Seek to have a week's worth of water on hand, as well as alternative sources of water and power, because the water source may be contaminated after a storm. The list also mentions keeping your property free from debris and other items that can be picked up in high winds and injure animals or harm their shelter. For more, see Livestock Disaster Preparedness on the United States Humane Society website. [7]

Be Aware and Be Prepared

You are out of town traveling internationally and become ill, and you will not be able to return to your home for weeks. Your pet sitter was booked for the original duration of the trip but is unable to handle your extended schedule. Who will you call to take care of your pets? Giving the best support to your pets requires you to understand their rights and your rights and to anticipate life changes that could disrupt their security. Plan for their protection. A trusted pet sitter is an amazing resource. You also need a backup plan.

In the discussion on the PETS Act, I mentioned that it does not cover some breeds of dogs. If you have a dog, do you know if it covers yours? If you have a rare snake or reptile or unusual pet, do not assume that state or federal emergency plans will include your pet. The best approach is for you to know. Research your local regulations so you can provide the best possible care.

If you are in the United States, it is very likely that your pet is still considered to be property. If you are with a partner and you divorce, the law does not consider the emotional well-being of your pet when awarding them to one party versus another. In January 2017, Alaska became the first state to create legislation that considers a pet's well-being during divorce proceedings. This act describes a pet as a "vertebrate living creature not a human being" rather than a piece of property. Illinois passed similar legislation in 2018, followed by California in 2019.[8]

Spain, France, Portugal, Germany, Switzerland, and Austria all have laws in place recognizing animals as sentient beings, capable of having emotions. As opposed to treating animal friends as possessions, they treat them more like underaged children. This means that when a couple splits, the law considers a pet's welfare and feelings. The partner who has greater financial solvency or, if applicable, receives custody of the children is more likely to receive custody of the pet. When there are children involved, the link between the children and the pet receives special consideration. [9]

If you live in a location where an animal is considered to be property and you share a pet with a partner, consider having a pet prenuptial agreement. For dogs, we might call that a pup prenup. Be clear about who keeps your furry, feathered, or scaly friend when the love is gone. Will you have joint custody? Write it down. And unless it is clear that one of you is walking away with 100 percent custody, discuss finances. Who is paying for the cat litter? What about visits to the veterinarian? This might sound petty, but if you find yourself in the middle of an ugly breakup, you could have drama over your pets. Or a judge might make a decision that you don't like. If you decide to create a pet prenuptial agreement, consider working with a local attorney to make sure you create something that is legally valid.

In the United States, even if you live in a location where your animal is considered property, many states allow you to create a trust for your pet. This means that you can legally set aside resources to care for your pet after you die. You cannot leave money or property directly to that pet, but you can set up a trust and assign someone to manage the trust with the legal understanding that they must use the resources to care for your pet. [10] A trust ensures that after your demise, your pet will be secure. If this approach appeals to you, make wise decisions as to who will oversee the trust. You want to assign someone who will love your special critter as much as you did. As with the pet prenuptial agreement, your best approach is to work with a legal professional.

Even if you do not set up a trust, you still want to have an agreement in place so that your pet will be cared for after you die. Make sure that you write this down and store it with your will and other instructions. Do not surprise anyone; talk to your friends and family to ensure that your designee is ready, willing, and able to take on the job. It is also a good idea to have a backup person.

Do you know what will happen to your furry, feathered, or scaly friend when you die? What if you become too ill to care for them, or what if you have to be away from home for an extended period of time? Being a responsible guardian means creating a safe future for your pet, even (or especially) when that future could be without you.

Adopt with Care

Last year, a friend of mine from a local meditation group adopted a puppy. Jim is in his midseventies and on the verge of retirement. When I think of a person who is grounded and secure, Jim's face comes to mind. He knows himself and owns his life. Jim joked that he figured he had about fifteen years of retirement money, so he could afford to live to be ninety. He also laughingly said that he wanted to name his dog Last Dog. (His wife was not amused, and they settled on a name that was agreeable to both of them.)

Is it fair to adopt an animal if you know that you will die first? You and the animal will form a bond. Other than knowing that all sentient beings are going to die, we do not know our exact time of death. Young people die. Middle aged people die. And old people die. I have had a nineteen-year-old cat, and when I was a child, our family puppy became ill and was dead before she was a year old. Love your pet while you can, and make sure that your pet will be cared for after you are gone.

The best thing you can do is to think before you adopt. I know that those kittens at the adoption fair are adorable. But before you pick one out and name him Sir Fluff A Lot, think. Is your lifestyle, and your living space right for a kitten? Kittens do not care if your furniture is expensive. Your couch might become a favorite climbing and scratching post. Will you move frequently? What will you do if you move into a location that is not pet friendly? Do you have close friends or a partner who is allergic to cats? What about other animals? Can you afford food, litter, and visits to the veterinarian? You are taking on responsibility for another life. You are becoming a *kahu*. A few years ago, I adopted a cat from a local cat rescue. I was equally surprised and impressed by the paperwork they required me to complete in order to adopt this little cat with the cute pink nose. I joked with a few of my friends that I felt like this paperwork was more detailed than if I had been adopting a human child. I still have a copy of the form, and I have included parts of it here so that you can see some of the details:

- Why are you looking for a cat?
- What kind of cat are you looking for (age, sex, breed, color)?
- List the names, ages, and relationship of everyone who shares your household other than co-applicant (kids, roommates).
- Does anyone in your household have allergies to animals?
- Who will be the cat's primary caregiver?
- If your current relationship were to change, with whom would the cat remain?

- How many hours of the day will your cat be left alone? Where will (s)he be left when alone? Will there be other animals with her/him when you are gone?
- How long have you lived at your current location?
- If condo or townhouse, what are the association's rules about keeping pets?
- Do you have any of the following: patio, balcony, pet door, unscreened windows or doors, back yard, front yard, other means of outdoor access?
- How much will the cat be exposed to cigarette smoke?
- None
    - Smoker in house
    - Smoker outside
- In what areas of your home will your cat be allowed?
- Where will you keep the litter box?
- Where will your cat sleep at night?
- What will you do if cat claws the drapes or furniture?
- What is a behavior that would not be acceptable to you?
- List all the pets who have recently been in your care.
- Will the adopted cat be indoors or outdoors?
- List the name and phone number of your veterinarian.
- How much would you be willing and able to spend on a medical emergency for your cat?

- What kind of food will you feed your cat?
- Who will take care of your cat when you are on vacation?
- Is there any reason you would no longer be able to care for your cat?

As I worked my way through the paperwork, I found myself moving away from annoyance to respect. This was an organization that really cared about the well-being of the cats in their care. This was not about dumping a cat on the first person who thought adopting a cat with a pink nose seemed like fun. After they reviewed my paperwork, we set an appointment for a representative to come to my house with the cat. I noticed that when she arrived, she left the cat in the carrier and asked if she could look around a bit. Then, she helped me find a location to help the cat feel secure as he settled in. She brought a blanket with him that had been his sleeping blanket. After we set him up, she made sure that she watched me interact with him. Then she left, with the request that I send her some updates, with pictures, over the next seventy-two hours to let her know how it was going. Later, I learned that this cat had rejected other humans and other households. He would not even let people pet him. Five years later, I am still his "hooman."

Before you make an impulse buy of a bird, turtle, lizard, or fish in the pet store, think. Don't bring that snake home until you really know that you are intending a long-term relationship. If you are going to attend a pet adoption fair, take the questions I have shared with you, and update them as appropriate. Be clear about your ability to adopt. There is a difference between the care required for a kitten versus an adult cat. Different dog breeds have different temperaments and needs. If you stumble upon some cute critters who are available for adoption before you are able to think things through, indicate your intention to adopt, and then exchange contact information and do your homework. If that specific pet is adopted before you are ready, do not worry. There will be another one. According to a study conducted by the Los Angeles Department of Animal Care and Control, there were approximately 60,000 stray dogs and 25,000 stray cats in Los Angeles County in 2023.[11] Somehow, I think these numbers might be conservative.

There is another option. Do not adopt a pet. In his article, "Want to truly have empathy for animals? Stop owning pets," Troy Vettese compares pet ownership with a theme from a short story by Ursula Le Guin. The story, "The Ones Who Walk Away from Omelas," tells of a society where the happiness of the citizens is dependent on the misery of one child who is kept in a dungeon. The philosophical question raised by this story is whether the torture of the child can be justified by the joy it brings to the rest of the community. Vettese draws comparisons between the imprisonment of the child and the way in which we keep pets.[12] He suggests that the best answer is to stop buying animals. His position is as follows:

> Pet ownership is bad for pets. The animals are harmed from the outset, regardless of whether they are sourced from puppy mills, the wild, or artisanal inbreeders. Often African grey parrots and other "exotics" are captured from their habitats, and many die en route to the market. Puppy mills are plagued by high mortality rates for the young, while mothers are kept perpetually pregnant

until they are discarded. Pedigreed animals, whose genetics are equivalent to the offspring of siblings, are often plagued by health problems during their truncated lives. [13]

Vettese makes many salient points as he rails against pet ownership. For example, if pets in the United States formed their own country, they would be fifth worldwide in terms of meat consumption. Many pets lead lives of loneliness. In Germany, the government issued a ruling that dogs must be walked for at least one hour per day. If dogs were receiving the attention required, such a measure would be unnecessary. And two in five African grey parrots pluck their feathers out of boredom. Vettese believes that when we have pets, we are taking animals and reducing them to the status of doll-like playthings. He advocates for a post-pet world, where we appreciate animals in their natural settings and respect them as autonomous beings. [14] It is hard to imagine that we will transition from our current pet-centric culture to the world Vettese envisions, yet we could do a better job ensuring that our pets receive quality care and attention. When I think of the premise behind "The Ones Who Walk Away from Omelas," I think of the pets who are adopted and ignored, the ones who receive food and water but nothing else. I would not say do not adopt; I would say do not adopt unless you are ready to go all in.

If you find that having a pet in your household is not right for you, consider volunteering at the animal rescue or shelter of your choice. There are many animals who can benefit from your time and attention. There are local groups who rescue specific species or specific breeds, and they are all clamoring for more hands and more resources. You can find a way to have a deep connection with our furry, feathered, or scaly friends without keeping one in your home.

Remember: They Are Animals

Most pets display so many humanlike traits and emotions it's easy to forget they're not gifted with the English language and then we get snubbed when we talk to them, and they don't say anything back. — Stephenie Geist

"It is like she is a toddler having a tantrum!" These are the words my mother used to describe the behavior of our family dog Pokey. Whenever we went away on vacation, Pokey dug up part of the garden. Not just any section of the garden. It was always the section my mother had most recently worked on. It did seem like Pokey was expressing her anger toward my mother. Eventually my mother worked on a fake gardening project before taking a trip so it did not matter if Pokey attacked it. Still, my mother acknowledged, "She is just a dog, and she is being a dog."

Our pets are not people. As much as we lean on them for support, affection, and companionship, we cannot expect them to respond like an actual human best friend. Their brain functions and nervous systems show us that they experience a range of emotions. They feel pleasure and pain. They remember people and places. [15]They know when you are driving them to the veterinarian's office. I had a friend who insisted that her dog understood the phrase "Aunt Margaret is coming over" and responded with joyful excitement. I had a cat who, upon seeing me cry, would come and inspect my tears and then curl up in my lap (of course, I cannot prove that he was trying to make me feel better).

We have no proof that animals make plans for their futures or contemplate their pasts. In "Goodbye Pixel," Julian Baggini considers the loss of his cat Pixel. He notes that it feels like losing a family member, yet he knows that it is not exactly the same. In seeking to clarify our relationship with animals, and the true nature of our roles, Baggini discusses the Maasai of Africa. They have deep bonds with the animals around them. They share names with their favorite oxen. Yet they recognize that they are different. And yes, they still slaughter and eat the animals around them. Baggini says:

> The ways in which all traditional societies have related to animals reflect how we humans are deeply embedded in the natural world, the kin of all living creatures. But they also recognize that every living creature is different and occupies its own place in the web of interdependence. To think of them all as friends and family would be naive and romantic. To recognize the value of nonhuman life for what it is requires acknowledging its real difference. [16]

As Baggini considers the relationship between pets and people, he says of his dying cat, "Pixel never had a single project in his life, an activity that required more than one session working at it to complete. He had only tasks: catch a mouse, eat, open the door, sharpen his claws on our furniture, curl up in any empty cardboard box left open." [17]

Baggini makes the case for us as the guardians of our pets. He would not agree that they are family members. He is not a fan of the term "pet parent." And he does view pets as property. He says, "It is an animal that we have taken stewardship of, enjoying what it offers us, and treating it with respect and care in return." He and his family loved Pixel. But he does not believe that Pixel loved them back. The relationship between them was asymmetric. Pixel had no responsibility for the well-being of his humans, but his humans had complete responsibility for Pixel's well-being. In a relationship with your pet, Baggini says, make no assumption of reciprocity or equality. [18]

Pay attention to your pets. They are dependent on your care. Years ago, my big fluffy cat Biff let me know that he was not feeling well. He did not cry, refuse to eat, or remain stationary. He followed me around the house, simply looking at me. Somehow, I knew that something was not right. Fortunately, the vet's office understood me when I said, "I don't know how to tell you how I know this, and I don't know what is wrong, but something is wrong." An exam revealed that he had a giant hairball in stomach. It was too large for him to cough up. By being present with him and mindful of his behavior, I realized something was wrong. We found the problem, and he lived for many years beyond that day. Several years later, I missed an event because I took a different cat to the emergency vet. A friend asked me, "How did you know?" And without even thinking about it I replied, "Because she told me." They don't speak like you, and I speak, but they do try to let us know when something is wrong. We are not always going to get it right, but we always need to pay them proper attention. If your animal companion is truly your friend, then get to know them like you would get to know a friend. Seek to understand their moods and changes in behavior. This is our responsibility. It is more than being happy to have them meet you at the door, sit on your lap, or take a walk with you.

Euthanasia

Imagine your beloved elderly dog, who has been your faithful companion for years, is now suffering, unable to eat or drink. He is listless, and occasionally whimpering. Your veterinarian advises you he is starting to experience organ failure. She suggests that it is time to think about euthanasia. You have loved your dog for many years. He has been a faithful companion and you have been his guardian and protector. What do you do?

It's hard to watch your pet suffer. And some of us have been taught that as a trusted caretaker, it is our duty to make the decision to end physical suffering. And when treatment no longer works, that can mean ending your pet's life with the assistance of your veterinarian. It seems compassionate to release them from suffering. And physical suffering is hard to bear.

You also have a responsibility to help them with their release from suffering at a higher level. The final moments of a sentient being influence their next rebirth. You know that an animal rebirth is undesirable. It takes more rebirths than we can count to move up to a higher realm. Even though animals are not able to comprehend the Dharma, they are still working with their karma. If you choose to end your dog's life, are you taking away his opportunity to have the type of death that would help him on his path toward liberation? Or if you let him continue to suffer until his natural death, will the pain he experiences and his response to that pain create more negative karma? What about the precept against killing? If you agree to euthanize your pet, you are choosing to end a life. This can create negative karma for you and your pet.

You are faced with your aversion to watching your loving dog go through physical suffering versus spiritual suffering. These moments of pain are shorter than the many lifetimes of animal rebirth. Yet in this moment you see the pain, you hear the cries, and you feel emotional anguish. The future rebirths can seem more intangible, and the ability to influence the karma of your dog can seem less concrete.

If you have pets, you will probably be faced with this decision. From a Buddhist perspective, there is no wiggle room. There is a precept against killing, and you do not want to interrupt your pet's cycle of karma. Here you are faced with an opportunity to strengthen your Buddhist practice. You are not joyful that your dog has immediate physical pain, and you are not apathetic about his future rebirth; you are appreciative of this chance to choose the Dharma. Because you have accepted this dog into your life and you have loved him, you are receiving the gift of the Dharma.

As an unenlightened human, I have had pets die from natural causes, and I have held the paws of others as, under my direction, the vet performed euthanasia.

If you decide against euthanasia, then work with your veterinarian to keep your pet as comfortable as possible. You might be able to take your pet to acupuncture or reiki or administer CBD ointments. Stay near your pet and offer reassurances and kind words. Keep food and water nearby. If your pet is unable to go outside or use a litter box, keep a pee pad close, and change it as often as possible. Think about what most sentient beings need during times of illness, and provide the equivalent for your cherished pet. Consider chanting. If you decide in favor of euthanasia, be sure that you are doing so with as pure a heart as possible. Do not euthanize your pet because you no longer want to care for them. Do not euthanize your pet because you cannot stand to be around suffering. Your decision must not be about what is best for you; it must be about what is best for your animal friend. Your choice must come from a place of being a *kahu*.

After your beloved pet passes away, whether naturally or through euthanasia, there are ways to help their spiritual journey. You can meditate, chant, and perform rituals with the goal of helping ease the way for a favorable rebirth. Consult with your own spiritual teacher for guidance.

Karma

In the chapter on animal rebirth, we discussed ways to help our animal friends create positive karma. We are responsible for our own karma, and so are the animals around us. Some say that animals are not really making choices. They believe that what animals experience is a type of evolutionary karma, meaning they do not create new karma; they simply continue to be reborn as animals until they have burned off old karma. Some of the teachings support this concept. Yet there are also *suttas* that tell of an animal being in the right place to create the conditions to have a better rebirth or performing a deed, such as guarding the Buddha while he meditated in the forest. In the instance of being in the right place to create conditions for a better rebirth, that could indicate that those conditions burned off the negative karma that was leading to rebirth in the animal realm. Choosing to perform an act seems to imply not just burning off old karma but also potentially creating new positive karma.

Whether your pet is burning off old karma or creating new karma, you have a responsibility to guide your furry, feathered, or scaly friend in a direction that leads to release from suffering. Consider caring for them a sacred responsibility, an expression of loving kindness and compassion. Feed them and play with them so that they do not need to hunt or to toy with other creatures. Give them toys that will engage their senses. Take them to training. Seek to place them in situations where they are most likely to exhibit non-harming behaviors.

Let's close with another quote from the 25th Tulku Rinpoche: "So taking care of pets is a spiritual journey and has been a spiritual practice for me. We need only understand that genuine Dharma practice is about benefiting all of those around us, whether two- or four-legged, and to realize that spiritual practice can be engaged anytime, anywhere, and with anyone." [19]

End Notes

[1] Simon, *The Dharma of Dogs*, 97.
[2] Tom [D-CA-12 Rep. Lantos, "H.R.3858 - 109th Congress (2005-2006): Pets Evacuation and Transportation Standards Act of 2006," legislation, October 6, 2006, 2005-09-22, http://www.congress.gov/bill/109th-congress/house-bill/3858.
[3] Erica LaVoy, "The PETS Act and Beyond: A Critical Examination of the PETS Act and What the Future of Disaster Planning and Response for Animals Should Be," *Mitchell Hamline Law Journal of Public Policy and Practice* 40, no. 1 (January 1, 2019), https://open.mitchellhamline.edu/policypractice/vol40/iss1/4.
[4] Rep. Lantos, "H.R.3858 - 109th Congress (2005-2006)."
[5] LaVoy, "The PETS Act and Beyond."
[6] https://www.facebook.com/onegreenplanet, "Help Make Sure Factory Farms Are Held Accountable for Leaving Animals to Die in Hurricane Florence," One Green Planet, October 1, 2018, https://www.onegreenplanet.org/news/factory-farms-held-accountable-leaving-animals-die-hurricane-florence/.
[7] "Livestock Disaster Preparedness," The Humane Society of the United States, accessed August 6, 2023, https://www.humanesociety.org/resources/livestock-disaster-preparedness.
[8] Bret Colson, "Pet Custody 101: Who Gets the Pets in a Divorce?," Survive Divorce, March 25, 2019, https://www.survivedivorce.com/pet-custody-divorce.
[9] Corina Pons and Corina Pons, "Dog Custody: Spain to Consider Pets' Welfare in Divorce Battles," *Reuters*, January 6, 2022, sec. Europe, https://www.reuters.com/world/europe/dog-custody-spain-consider-pets-welfare-divorce-battles-2022-01-05/.
[10] "How Animals Differ from Other Types of 'Property' Under the Law," *Animal Legal Defense Fund* (blog), accessed August 6, 2023, https://aldf.org/article/how-animals-are-treated-differently-from-other-types-of-property-under-the-law/.
[11] "Los Angeles County Animal Care," accessed August 6, 2023, https://animalcare.lacounty.gov/.
[12] Troy Vettese, "Want to Truly Have Empathy for Animals? Stop Owning Pets," *The Guardian*, February 4, 2023, sec. Opinion, https://www.theguardian.com/commentisfree/2023/feb/04/want-to-truly-have-empathy-for-animals-stop-owning-pets.
[13] Vettese.
[14] Vettese.
[15] "What I Think about When I Say Goodbye to My Beloved Dying Pet | Aeon Essays."
[16] "What I Think about When I Say Goodbye to My Beloved Dying Pet | Aeon Essays."

[17] "What I Think about When I Say Goodbye to My Beloved Dying Pet | Aeon Essays."
[18] "What I Think about When I Say Goodbye to My Beloved Dying Pet | Aeon Essays."
[19] Simon, *The Dharma of Dogs*, 97.

Chapter 9

More Pets, More Attachment

The difference between friends and pets is that friends we allow into our company, pets we allow into our solitude. – **Robert Brault**

It is in that solitude where our true selves emerge. Our pets see and hear things that no other will know. There is no hidden agenda, no need for pretense. When we close the door, when we disconnect from others, we allow them to be part of our entire world. We develop bonds that are deeper and stronger than the bonds we have with some of our human family. We are attached to our pets. Let's look at some of the data, and then we will connect with some of our Buddhist teachings.

In June 2023, Consumer Affairs conducted a survey that uncovered how strongly millennials felt about their pets (you are a millennial if you were born between 1981 and 1996). Eighty-one percent of millennials surveyed stated they loved their pet more than at least one family member. Now you are probably wondering which family member. Who is less popular than a millennial's pet?

- 57% said they loved their pet more than they loved their brothers and/or sisters.
- 50% said they loved their pet more than they loved their mother.
- 41% said they loved their per more than they loved their father.
- 31% said they loved their pet more than they loved their grandparents.
- 30% said they loved their pet more than they loved their partners,
- 12% said they loved their pet more than they loved their cousins. [1]

Are you the parent of a millennial child? If you are waiting for grandchildren, you might need to wait longer or become comfortable with the idea of a grand-cat or grand-dog. Why? Because 58 percent of millennials would rather have pets than children.

That's millennials. So what? In 2023, millennials made up the biggest segment of the population in the United States. They are driving the pet-based economy and the culture. Millennials are setting the trends for many things, including the overall relationship with pets in our society.[2]

Gen Z, born between 1997 and 2012, is following in their footsteps. A survey conducted by Zillow found that members of Gen Z would prioritize the needs of pets over partners when considering where to live.[3] If you want your millennials or Gen Z children to live near you, then make sure you let them know how that your neighborhood is very pet friendly. Why? Because 86 percent of them will not move without considering how it impacts their animal friend.[4]

It is not just the millennials and Gen Z. As of 2023, 66 percent of US households own a pet. And while millennials are the largest group, baby boomers account for 24 percent of the total. And 78 percent of those who participated acquired a pet during the pandemic.

We reach out to animals for companionship. [5] And when those relationships do not go as planned, or when it is time for them to end, we encounter the Noble Truth of Suffering.

The Truth of Suffering

The Buddha's first teaching was called the *Dhammacakkappavattana Sutta*, which means the Turning of the Wheel of Truth. He gave this discourse to the five ascetics who were his former companions at the Deer Park in Isipatana (now called Sarnath), near Benares, India.

The Buddha started by advising the five ascetics to give up two extremes—specifically, indulgence in sensual pleasures and the tormenting of the body (self-indulgence and self-mortification). He selected these two extremes because too much sensual pleasure is not noble and is not helpful in spiritual development. On the other hand, tormenting the body is painful, not noble, and also unhelpful in spiritual development. He advised them to follow the Middle Way. It was during this teaching that the Buddha taught the Four Noble Truths. They are the truth of suffering, its cause, its end, and the way to its end. You probably recall this from our discussion in Chapter 3: Animal Rebirth.

This first teaching was not a practice session. He did not start with some throw-away lesson just to see who was listening. He had a profound experience, and he woke up and saw the truth of our existence.

Now let's fast forward. The Buddha taught for about forty years and then died. He obtained nirvana and was no longer subject to rebirth. Why? Because he gained release from suffering. He did not cling; he did not experience aversion.

Consider his body of teaching, the thousands of lessons he taught, the thousands of lessons his monks taught. Why? What was the reason? To show us how to live in a way that we could also gain release from suffering.

Consistently, the Buddha and his followers taught how to live good lives, do no harm, act with compassion, and develop equanimity. There are also some very deep teachings on dependent origination and form and consciousness. He did not teach us so that we could sit on a cushion and develop psychic powers. He taught us so that we could transcend suffering.

The basics, such as the idea of the Four Noble Truths, are easy to comprehend. That does not make them easy to carry out. The Buddha was a skillful teacher. He knew this was difficult, so he presented it to us using many similes, seeking to help us to understand. He wanted us to engage in the practice.

It is attachment that makes the difference. Attachment makes it difficult for us to let go of our beloved pets. Attachment leads us to consider clones, taxidermy, or lookalike plushies. And it is attachment that, per the second Noble Truth, causes us suffering.

Transferring Attachment to Pets

When someone you love dies, moves away, or cuts off contact from you, it hurts. You miss them. You miss the prospect of spending more time together. It's difficult to know that there will be no more walks, or scratching their ears, or playing fetch. Yes, I am discussing when that someone is your animal friend. In the Buddha's time, relationships with animals were different than today. The teachings around loss of a loved one assumed the death of a human friend of family member. But if you are a millennial and you love your pet more than you love some of your family members, your strongest attachment may be to a furry, feathered, or scaly critter.

To elaborate on the truth of suffering, you control your own level of stress or dissatisfaction through clinging and aversion. This is not a statement of blame; this is simply an observation of what it means to be human. It is like this:

> Whatever stress, in arising, arose for me in the past, all of it had desire as its root, had desire as its cause—for desire is the cause of stress. And whatever stress, in arising, will arise for me in the future, all of it will have desire as the root, will have desire as its cause—for desire is the cause of stress. (SN 42.11)

Having to face the impermanence of your pet, to know that you will outlive that pet, and to wish for a different outcome. That can be the truth of your suffering. In the *Gandhabhaka Sutta,* the Buddha walked Gandhabhaka the headman through some of the finer points of impermanence, attachment, and stress. The primary message in this teaching is about attachment. And this attachment became clear when Gandhabhaka was faced with the impermanence of others.

> The Blessed One said: "Now what do you think, headman: Are there any people in Uruvelakappa who, if they were murdered or imprisoned or fined or censured, would cause sorrow, lamentation, pain, distress, or despair to arise in you?"
>
> "Yes, lord, there are people in Uruvelakappa who, if they were murdered or imprisoned or fined or censured, would cause sorrow, lamentation, pain, distress, or despair to arise in me."
>
> "And are there any people in Uruvelakappa who, if they were murdered or imprisoned or fined or censured, would cause no sorrow, lamentation, pain, distress, or despair to arise in you?"
>
> "Yes, lord, there are people in Uruvelakappa who, if they were murdered or imprisoned or fined or censured, would cause no sorrow, lamentation, pain, distress, or despair to arise in me."
> (SN 42.11)

Every instance of the death or misfortune of others does not hold the same level of stress for Gandhabhaka. This teaching does not give us any reason to believe that he actively wished for the death or misfortune of anyone. Just that there are some people whose demise would be more painful for him. With the arising of compassion and equanimity, his experience would be different. But this is not the purpose of the teaching. On this occasion, Gandhabhaka had specifically asked the Buddha to teach him the origin and ending of stress. And to make sure that Gandhabhaka is understanding the lesson, the Buddha continued:

Now what is the cause, what is the reason, why the murder, imprisonment, fining, or censure of some of the people in Uruvelakappa would cause you sorrow, lamentation, pain, distress, or despair, whereas the murder imprisonment, fining, or censure of others would cause you no sorrow, lamentation, pain, distress, or despair?

Those people in Uruvelakappa whose murder, imprisonment, fining, or censure would cause me sorrow, lamentation, pain, distress, or despair are those for whom I feel desire and passion. Those people in Uruvelakappa whose murder, imprisonment, fining, or censure would cause me no sorrow, lamentation, pain, distress, or despair are those for whom I feel no desire or passion. (SN 42.11)

The difference is the depth of Gandhabhaka's feelings. To make this even more clear, the Buddha asked how Gandhabhaka would feel if his son were to experience death or misfortune. The Buddha also asked how Gandhabhaka would feel if his wife experienced death or misfortune. And in both cases Gandhabhaka acknowledged that he would be devastated. Today, if the Buddha had that discussion with a millennial, he would be contrasting the love of a pet to the love of a brother, sister, mother, father, or grandparents. The key message is the same, but the beings who lead us to feel sorrow, lamentation, pain, distress, or despair are different.

The question arises: if we have turned our attachment toward our animal companions, are we turning away from other human beings?

Aversion to Humans?

Having pets often provides significant rewards with relatively low effort. While pets require attention, food, and shelter, their demands are generally easier to meet than with human companions. Sure, your discussion with your ferret is one-sided. But if you enjoy petting and playing and talking with your ferret, then it might be a worthwhile tradeoff. If you like sharing your space but do not live with family or friends and perhaps do not want to live with family or friends, then a pet really helps to meet your needs. If you do not want a human roommate, a pet is an excellent alternative. A pet will help you stave off loneliness and depression. A pet, especially a dog, will give you unconditional love.

I once heard the head of a large organization dedicated to rehabilitating formerly incarcerated gang members state that if his nonprofit rescued puppies or if they could use puppies in their advertising, they would double the amount of donations they received. He also felt that people cared more about displaced puppies and kittens than they cared about people trying to rebuild their lives. Was he right? We might be hard-wired to love animals and, in some cases, to care about the well-being of animals over other adult humans. Researchers Jack Levin, Arnold Arluke, and Leslie Irvine examined whether people are more emotionally disturbed by reports of abuse to non-human animals than to similar reports of abuse to humans.

> Two hundred and fifty-six under-graduates at a major northeastern university were asked to indicate their degree of empathy for a brutally beaten human adult or child versus an adult dog or puppy, as described in a fictitious news report. We hypothesized that the vulnerability of victims—determined by

their age and not species—would determine participants' levels of distress and concern for them. The main effect for age but not for species was significant. We also found more empathy for victims who are human children, puppies, and fully-grown dogs than for victims who are adult humans. Age makes a difference for empathy toward human victims, but not for dog victims. In addition, female participants were significantly more empathic toward all victims than were their male counterparts. [6]

Is it true that advertisements featuring puppies and kittens elicit more of a response? And would the picture of a dog lead to more interest? The answer to these questions inspired a nonprofit in the United Kingdom to test two different versions of the same advertisement. In 2015, the nonprofit ran two ads. Both featured this text: "Would you give £5 to save Harrison from a slow, painful death?" Both were for Harrison's Fund and were meant to solicit donations for a young boy who had Duchenne muscular dystrophy. Where the ads differed was in the image used alongside the text. One showed the picture of the actual eight-year-old boy. The other featured an image of a dog. The picture of the dog received 230 clicks, while the one with the boy received 111 clicks. The report did not include the actual donation amount attributed to each.[7]

None of this means that dogs and other animals will always garner more concern. We can be very inconsistent when it comes to our treatment of animals. We still use them for their hides and for food. There is still animal testing. Some think of the animals around them as property. Consider guard dogs, who are a form of security system. When we feel more empathetic toward animals, it is often toward species that have been anthropomorphized or are considered to be more intelligent, possibly less wild, and, of course, cute. [8]

We do still see that pets and humans are not exactly the same. In the study cited above, human infants received the highest amount of concern. Respondents may feel care or responsibility to those who are similar, which may explain why there was more concern for the human baby than for the puppy. However, the baby and the puppy both elicited more empathy than the human adult, which may indicate that vulnerability is also an important factor. Other studies on human empathy have found that empathy can be a programmed response to ensure that the young receive protection. They do represent survival of the species. [9]

The researchers proposed another possibility: the participants viewed the adult human as capable of removing themselves from the abusive situation, where a young child, a puppy, or a dog might not be able to defend themselves or escape. [10] If this is true, then it does help to support the concept of pets as children or as dependent family members. For those unable to rescue themselves, we take on the role of their caretaker. And you can be a caretaker for one without turning your back on the other.

Another theory is that there has been a "collapse of compassion." This psychological principle asserts that the more tragedy we see, the less we care. When we are subjected to the suffering of more and more people, we begin to lose our compassion. Internally, we build a wall to help to protect us from feeling overwhelmed or afraid. When you experience a "collapse of compassion," you might find yourself unable to care about the suffering of a large group of people. You learn that a major earthquake has killed or displaced thousands of people, and you are unable to feel concerned. But you see a news story of one injured child, and you burst into tears or donate to a fund to assist that child and their family. [11] In a world where we have access to news 24/7 and so much of that news involves difficult things happening to many people, it just might be easier to turn away from people and turn toward our animal friends.

If we are not careful, we can let this "collapse of compassion" turn us way from helping other humans. I am not saying set aside your feelings for your pets. In difficult times, it helps to be able to shower some affection on an innocent creature. Walking in nature or petting your animal friend may help decrease your anxiety. But be mindful of actively becoming aversive to other human beings. You can love your animal and still carry feelings of compassion for your own species. Be aware of a mindset that decreases your ability to care for others or even pits you against them.

Skillful Attachment

There are animals who come into our lives because it is their job to help us. This is the case with service dogs. There are dogs who learn to recognize the signs of an oncoming seizure, dogs who can detect that your blood sugar is too high or too low, dogs who help with anxiety, and dogs who help with mobility. Because their job is to help us, we form special bonds with them. An attachment. This is the case with Anne and Inga (not their real names). Inga is a service dog who helps her human, Anne, with mobility issues. Anne has degenerative disc disease, which makes movement, such as getting up and down difficult, almost impossible. Ann was kind enough to speak with me about her relationship with Inga.

One of the first questions I asked Anne was whether she saw Inga as a pet or as a family member or primarily as a working dog. Without hesitation, Anne replied that Inga was absolutely her friend. If she had to list her five closest friends, Inga would be on that list. As her helper, Inga is a companion, and that bond is not just a bond of obligation; it is built on trust and affection, on both sides. In fact, when Anne described how Inga enhances her life, she mentioned companionship. This is a relationship that goes beyond helping to prevent Anne from falling.

Anne admires Inga's intelligence, and she caters to her needs. This is not a one-sided relationship. Of course, Inga needs food and shelter. She also likes to be active and engaged. Anne has taken her through training programs, has play time with her, and responds when Inga seeks out cuddles and affection.

Some service dogs come almost fully trained. But this was not the case with Inga. A fully trained dog is very expensive. For Anne, these costs were not covered by insurance. Inga came with the proper disposition to be a service dog. In fact, she was learning how to be a diabetic alert dog. Inga is a German shepherd, and Anne has experience training this breed. Anne taught Inga the basic obedience commands: sit, stay, down, etc. Without mastering these commands, Inga could not be out in public. If Anne wants to go to a movie, Inga needs to be able to stay down and in place next to Anne until it is time to get up.

Together, Anne and Inga have built on the basics. Inga understands commands in German and English. In the United States, it is less likely that a German speaker will approach Inga and try to interact with her. Inga knows to stay close and to come around to the left side, or to stand in front of Anne. Brace means to stand in place and create a solid base so that Anne can stand up without losing her balance. Inga can retrieve things in a way that is different than playing fetch. She can open doors. And she can use straps attached to drawer handles to open drawers. All of these abilities, and the aptitude and attitude to use them to help Anne, make Inga a helpful and caring companion.

One of the reasons I spoke with Anne about her experience with Inga is that Anne is a practicing Buddhist. We talked about how her Buddhist practice integrates with her relationship with Inga. Anne has practiced for several years, and in some ways, this makes it difficult for her to identify how Buddhism shows up in her relationship with Inga. That being said, Anne knows that mindfulness has been a key component. Inga is a highly sensitive and intelligent dog. It has been essential for Anne to pay close attention to how she instructs her because Inga notices inconsistencies in her training. Inga has needs: the need for attention, intellectually stimulation, and physical activity. Anne pays close attention to Inga in order to understand how and when to meet these needs. Inga is not a robotic dog. She is a sentient being.

Anne and Inga have a genuine affection for one another. And that means attachment. They are both aging. It is possible that Anne will outlive Inga. Their relationship provides Anne with an opportunity to work with impermanence. The idea of losing Inga can bring Anne to tears. They have a closeness that transcends many other relationships. Together, they have shared many moments, and each has dedicated her time, energy, and devotion to the other. Anne turns to the *brahmavihārā,* the four immeasurables, for guidance. The combination of loving kindness, compassion, sympathetic joy, and equanimity assist her in accepting that impermanence is neither good nor bad; it simply is the true nature of things. In dealing with the Noble Truth of suffering, a little compassion can go a long way. In speaking with Anne, I was struck by the skillful way in which she dealt with her attachment to Inga.

We do not all need a service dog, but we do all need special relationships to live a life that is meaningful, to have a sense of fulfillment. Avoiding attachment does mean cutting off your feelings for others. It is not bad that you love your furry, feathered, or scaly critter. Work to be aware of how feelings of attachment and aversion surface for you. And since we are not practicing in complete solitude, interacting with our pets is a critical opportunity for us to practice mindfulness, equanimity, compassion, and loving kindness.

Plenty of Practice

Everyday life gives us our opportunity for practice. All we have to do is pay attention to engage. Life comes along and says to us, "Oh, you thought you were going to have an easy commute today? No, you are not. Guess what. Your car is breaking down." Or "Oh, you thought you were getting promoted today? Guess what. You are getting laid off." Or conversely, "Guess what. We are offering you a better position."

You know the Four Noble Truths. Do you know them intellectually, or do you know them in your heart? Is the truth of suffering front and center in your life? And have you considered how your attachment to your animal friends contributes to the truth of suffering? The more important our relationships with our animal friends, and the more that we think of them as family and love them as family, the more difficult it will be when they die.

Ultimately, it's "Oh, you thought you would live forever?" or "Oh, you thought this dog would always be by your side?" Nope! That's our recognition of death, and that is the ultimate impermanence. With it can come the biggest or most intense clinging or aversion you might ever experience. As we acknowledge our attachment, as we come to face to face with it, we sit with it, greet it by name, and come closer to our release from suffering. And that is what it is all about. This is the purpose of our practice.

End Notes

[1] "Pets Are Family: Survey | ConsumerAffairs®," June 1, 2023, https://www.consumeraffairs.com/pets/pets-are-family.html.

[2] "Resident Population in the United States in 2023, by Generation," accessed August 6, 2023, https://www.insiderintelligence.com/charts/united-states-population-by-generation/.

[3] "Gen Z Would Prioritize Pets over Partners and Kids If Buying a Home - Apr 11, 2023," Zillow MediaRoom, accessed August 6, 2023, https://zillow.mediaroom.com/2023-04-11-Gen-Z-would-prioritize-pets-over-partners-and-kids-if-buying-a-home.

[4] "Pets Are Family."

[5] "Pet Ownership Statistics and Facts in 2023 – Forbes Advisor."

[6] Jack Levin, Arnold Arluke, and Leslie Irvine, "Are People More Disturbed by Dog or Human Suffering? Influence of Victim's Species and Age," *Society and Animals* 25 (April 18, 2017), https://doi.org/10.1163/15685306-12341440.

[7] Levin, Arluke, and Irvine.

[8] Levin, Arluke, and Irvine.

[9] Levin, Arluke, and Irvine.

[10] Levin, Arluke, and Irvine.

[11] "Steering Clear of Compassion Collapse," Center for Compassionate Leadership, April 21, 2023, https://www.centerforcompassionateleadership.org/blog/steering-clear-of-compassion-collapse.

Chapter 10

Our Pets and Our Practice

"**I** never want to have another dog again." The woman sitting next to me was adamant. I was a bit surprised at the strength of her declaration, first because we did not know one another, and second because we live in such a pet-centric society. It was an interesting declaration to make in a neighborhood where many shops and restaurants have water bowls and treats at the ready for the steady stream of dogs walking by with their humans.

"It is too hard," she continued. "You get to know them. You learn to love them, and then they die. I don't think I can say goodbye to one more dog." And then I began to understand her perspective. In a world where we might keep physical and emotional distance from other human beings, we are attached to our pets. Our dogs, cats, birds, fish, and reptiles are our friends and family members.

As we discussed in Chapter 9: More Pets, More Attachment, the grief that comes with the loss when this bond is broken is intense. The choice that this woman was making was not to engage. Loving a sentient being without attachment is difficult. This is why you can find various quotes that associate grief as part of love or grief as the price of love. One quote says that grief is love with no place to go, all the love you have stored up for a sentient being who is now gone.

In most cases, to love a pet is to know that you will outlive that pet. To live with a pet is to observe the cycle of aging and death. I have had the benefit of being part of this journey with more than one cat. And one, a cat named Alex, really taught me about aging. She left me with an understanding that being open and flexible to whatever comes my way is the key to aging gracefully.

Alex the Aging Coach

Alex's resilience was amazing. When her companion cat died, Alex went through a very rough patch. She lost weight, and her fur fell out. She was grieving. I began to realize that she, too, would soon be gone. Soon actually ended up being two and a half years later. And during that time, I began to look at her as my aging coach or mentor. She showed me what it was like to be an old lady. Watching her experience the challenges of aging, I was amazed at the grace and dignity with which she navigated her days. Some days, she would look at me as if to say, "Can you believe this?" But she forged ahead, making every day her own.

As she aged, Alex either ate or she did not. Some days nothing would entice to her eat. One evening she practically assaulted one of my friends over a cupcake. It's about the balance between extremes. I do not recall too many days when she snacked. The good news was that until her last week, the not eating versus the eating remained in balance. I recall watching my mother-in-law go through something very similar. Some days she would tell me that everything was too salty. Other days she would clean her plate and reach across to finish mine. Her weight was consistent until the week before she died.

Alex never knew herself to be anything other than a pretty cat. Even when her fur fell out and she had a bald stripe down her back, I told her she was a pretty girl. And she looked at me, blinked, and rubbed her head against my hand. No matter how old you get and how much your looks change, to someone you will be beautiful. Accept compliments and affection with grace. Let friends and loved ones shower you with hugs and compliments. It's good for all of you.

Logically, we know that things are going to change. Parts of your body will work differently or not at all. At some point, Alex lost her hearing. I don't know exactly when it happened. I discovered it after her companion cat died. One day, Alex just started screaming, and as much as I called to her, she did not respond. I realized that she had relied on her companion cat as her hearing guide. Eventually we both adjusted. I learned that if I needed her attention, I could thump on the floor with my foot, and she would feel the vibrations and respond. She learned that she could meow at me like always, and I would respond. She adapted to her hearing limitation and kept going.

As a young cat, Alex loved to go outdoors. She had no intention of becoming an indoor cat. In the last couple of years, she went next door to eat the neighbor's grass, did a lap around her yard, and then came in. In her last year, she went to eat the neighbor's grass, came back, lay in the sun, and then came in. In her last few weeks, she went go outside, sniffed the air, lay down in the sun, and came back in within ten minutes. Seek to continue to enjoy fresh air, sunlight, good company, and beautiful art and music that brings you joy for as long as you can. You could lament the fact that you can no longer run a 10k, or you could get out and walk up and down the sidewalk. Or sit in the front yard. The choice is yours; the clock is ticking.

As Alex aged, she needed digestive aids, special medicine, and more than one type of special food. She drank lactose-free milk. She did not always hit the litter box. And she had no problem waking me up to let me know that she needed something. None of this gave her any concern. And it should not bother you either. You are here, and you are doing your best.

Live your life to the fullest, and make every moment count. On more than on occasion, I thought that Alex was at death's door. She rallied several times. I joked with friends that the Grim Reaper would come, and Alex would start to follow him. Then she would stop and say, "Hey, wait a minute. I am a cat. I have nine lives. Read the contract, buddy. It's not time yet." We do not have nine lives, but we do have the ability to maximize our time. Live until you have no more life left to live. And if you decide to share that life with a pet, let that pet become part of your practice. Learn how to love without (or with less) attachment, and learn how to age and how to live until you die.

Alex, Soho, Maple, and *Dukkha*

Alex taught me so much. She showed up as a stray and insisted on moving in. She made friends with our younger cat, Maple, but not our older cat, Soho. She tried to stay away from Soho, but the friction between them caused Alex to exhibit unpleasant signs of anxiety. She marked paper, clothing, and pillows. One time she marked me. But she stayed.

The truth is there is suffering or dissatisfaction. Soho was not happy that Alex invaded his territory. Maple would not play with Alex once Soho asserted his dominance. And we were not happy to find Alex urinating all over the house. All the sentient beings in the house wanted some things to stay the same and the difficult things to stop being difficult. I am pretty sure that Soho wanted Alex to disappear. I think Maple did not want to feel torn between Alex and Soho, and eventually she chose to follow Soho, the alpha. Alex wanted a safe and comfortable home and cuddles. Ed and I wanted cats who did not urinate outside the litter box.

The third truth is there is a way out of dissatisfaction. I do not think the cats were capable of following the Noble Eightfold Path, but Ed and I did our best. Ultimately, impermanence came along: Soho died, and overnight Alex became a model cat.

By using cats to tell this story, I am not denigrating the Four Noble Truths. I am pointing out that if you really pay attention to the animals in your life, the roles they play, and your interactions with them, there is so much that you can apply to your practice. We have much to learn.

Perfect Teachers?

Many of the teachers I interviewed for *Sitting with Death: Buddhist Insights to Help You Face Your Fears and Live a Peaceful Life* shared that their first experiences with death came from childhood and the death of a family pet. One teacher grew up in Alaska. Her observations went beyond the loss of a pet. Not all the animal deaths that she observed were the result of hunting or fishing. Some were more natural effects of the life cycles of animals living in the wild.

Helping us to understand aging, death, and impermanence is more than enough, and yet, our pets have provided more valuable lessons. Sometimes a cat or in this story, a dog is the perfect teacher. One evening while contemplating the phrase, "In each moment of life, we are creating who we are," Susanna Weiss found herself wondering how to move forward. Who would be her teacher? And then she realized she had the perfect teacher. His name was the Artful Dodger, and he was a golden retriever. Not just any golden retriever. Dodger loved people and had a special gift for recognizing those who most needed to feel loved. He might see someone from a block away and know that he wanted to greet that human. And invariably that human walked away with a smile and a glow. In fact, Susanna credits Dodger with teaching her to watch and listen (Dodger also sniffed, but that is not typically received well in a human-to-human interaction). This silent, deep presence allowed her to offer her chaplaincy patients the ability to open up and release what they needed to release. [1]

Beryl Bender Birch owes Hopi the Siberian Husky for reminding her of the essence of her spiritual practice. Watching Hopi navigate life joyfully while dealing with terminal cancer was a continual lesson in paying attention to your surroundings, being in the new, and appreciating every walk and every opportunity to play. We are all subject to impermanence. [2]

In the *Udayi Sutta* (AN 5.159), the Buddha explains to Ānanda the difficulties in teaching the Dharma. He shares the five qualities possessed by a true Dharma teacher:

1. To speak step by step.
2. To speak explaining the sequence of cause and effect.
3. To speak out of compassion.
4. To not speak for material reward.
5. To speak without hurting myself and others.

It is important to be careful in naming our animal companions as teachers. A true Dharma teacher is an advanced spiritual practitioner, someone who has developed virtue, purity, endurance, and discernment. We already know that our pets are in the animal realm because they are working off negative karma. We know that they may have moments of endurance or appear to be virtuous, but they are not. There may be moments when we think we see them exhibiting discernment, but this is us wanting to endow them with human attributes. We can absolutely learn from them, but it is not reasonable to call them Dharma teachers. Animals are our Dharma companions. In their company, we can learn. These animals we meet on the path can play a crucial role in our spiritual development.

We have already seen how a cat can show you what it is like to age gracefully, or how anger and resentment can lead to *dukkha*. Here are a few more lessons from other humans and their Dharma companions.

Get Back to Gratitude

Orange the cat helped Rachel Naomi Remen get back in touch with her own gratitude practice. Rachel suffered from Crohn's disease. To manage her wellness, she had a very limited diet and frequently ate the same foods over and over again. She found herself resenting her repetitive diet and the condition that required her special eating regime. One day, after preparing a bowl of tuna for Orange, Rachel paused and watched. Orange stood in front of his bowl with his eyes closed. He purred for a short time, and then he leaned forward and ate. It was almost as if Orange was offering thanks for his food. Orange was very happy to eat the same thing at each meal. Rachel understood that she, too, could be appreciative of each meal. And she wondered how else she was making her own experience more difficult. [3]

It's Your Path. Own It

From Ziggy the cat, Stéphane Garnier adopted an approach to problem-solving. After a serious accident, Ziggy had a paw amputated. Ziggy took this in stride, learning to adapt and move on. Watching Ziggy, Stéphane devised a decision-making process. Would he approach a particular situation or challenge from the front? Maybe he would circle it? Take higher ground? Ziggy might also reevaluate the issue and act indifferent. Or confront the issue. In some instances, Ziggy would stubbornly hold his ground. The theme behind Ziggy's selections seemed to be, "Follow your instincts, and act in a way that advances your well-being and your happiness." [4] That is some solid advice. As life brings you challenges, you get to decide how to meet them: head on, sideways, or not at all. Make choices that help you conquer suffering.

It's about Love

Maybe the most important lesson, the one that really allows us to access all of the other lessons, is love. In *The Dharma of Dogs,* Lama Tsomo tells of her experience with her dog Kusung. She says, "Love is her superpower. Lost love hasn't dimmed it; self-justification hasn't dimmed it; her capacity to give and receive love remains constant and limitless. In watching Kusung, I receive a long deep lesson in simply loving—fully open-heartedly, no matter what."

It really is about love. [5] Or as Zephyr the dog says, "Know that the world is overwhelmingly filled with love, except for vacuum cleaners—those are inherently evil." [6]

Now It Is Up To You

The vital function that pets fulfill in this world hasn't been fully recognized.

They keep millions of people sane.

When you pet a dog, or listen to a cat purring, thinking may subside for a moment.

And a space of stillness arises within you, a doorway into Being. –
Eckhart Tolle

You have the ability to recognize the vital function that your pet fulfills. To let your pet help you unlock your own spiritual potential. You are going to love them and live with them and perhaps consider yourselves to be family. Learn the difference, and be aware of the choice you are making and why. You have seen that pet ownership has mostly been for the privileged. This was true in the time of the Buddha, and it is true based on the statistics you have read for today. If you want to shower your pet with toys, hats, and costumes, great! But please consider who you are making happy with these activities. Maybe some of your pet toy budget could be donated to a shelter to help pets who are less fortunate than yours. Remember we are the guardians of the animals around us. If you subscribe to the beliefs around rebirth presented earlier, then you know that you have probably been an animal, and your friends and family have been animals, just as the Buddha lived many lives as various animals before he came to be an enlightened teacher.

Your lessons might be similar to those discussed in this chapter or in this book, or they might be completely different. When you open your heart, your home, and your practice to a pet or to the animals around you, there is no limit to what you might reveal. With pure attention, compassion, and the intention to let go of ego, who knows where your Dharma companion will take you.

End Notes

[1] Simon, *The Dharma of Dogs*, 91–93.
[2] Simon, *The Dharma of Dogs*. 161.
[3] Diana Ventimiglia, ed., *The Karma of Cats: Spiritual Wisdom from Our Feline Friends: An Anthology* (Boulder, Colorado: Sounds True, 2019), 38–40.
[4] Ventimiglia, 105–9.
[5] Simon, *The Dharma of Dogs*, 35.
[6] Simon, 39.
[7] Simon, 160.

Conclusion

When you read the Jātakas, you encountered stories where animals may show wisdom or ethical behavior. These stories teach us how the Bodhisatta became the Buddha. Not all Jātakas are animal stories. But there are enough animal stories to see how the inclusion of animals is a skillful teaching device—a valuable way to teach us Buddhism and morality and how to live. You do not have to accept rebirth to benefit from these stories. Each one has a self-contained lesson and a reminder that the journey to enlightenment is long, arduous, and achievable. In many of the Jātakas, the Buddha begins by saying, "When I was just an unenlightened *bodhisatta...*" This shows that there is hope for those of us who are unenlightened.

You can learn from watching the animals around you. In most instances, your animal friends are not intentionally choosing admirable behaviors, yet you can still observe them and use your discernment to take away lessons to apply to your own experience. In fact, I think that because their behavior is often so uncomplicated, it is easier to find a lesson. A cat does not pretend to like you. A dog only approaches certain people.

If you are fortunate, you will have a special relationship with an animal. Perhaps more than one. I have loved each cat who has been part of my life over the past several years. Each relationship has been different. Some have had deeper bonds and understanding or felt like closer friendships. Some may have existed to teach me patience or to help me develop feelings of love and compassion to those I find to be difficult.

Love your pet, and enjoy your time together. Do not forget that your time together is finite. It is the temporary nature of your relationship that can make it so sweet. Be mindful of the expectations you create around your life and relationship with your pet, and acknowledge where you have attachment. As much as you lean on them for support, affection, and companionship, your pets are not people.

In Buddhist cosmology, animals have a place. They are not as fortunate as humans. Their lives are shorter and more traumatic. Because they have unfortunate rebirths and difficult lives, we must do our best to treat them with kindness and compassion. As you go about your life, showering your pet with attention, special food, toys, and comfortable bedding, think about how you can help them burn off the karma that brought them to the animal realm. That is the real gift you can give: to move beyond what makes us happy about having a pet and seek to find ways that improve their existence at a level above material things. Our behavior toward animals and others will shape our karma.

We are human, and we will fall short. And it is our karma that determines our rebirths and our ultimate freedom from suffering. Or as the *Upajjhatthana Sutta* reminds us, "I am the owner of my actions, heir to my actions, born of my actions, related through my actions, and have my actions as my arbitrator. Whatever I do, for good or for evil, to that will I fall heir." (AN 5.57)

Your furry, feathered, and scaly companions have admirable qualities, and being their guardian will help you to learn and grow. Just as some of the Tibetan Buddhist deities have animal companions by their sides, you have the opportunity to include pets and the other animals around you on your journey. You can learn from their ability to live in the moment. You can seek to be as forgiving as many of them are, and you can greet your loved ones with joy. Offering care and guardianship to another sentient being is admirable, especially if you do so with no expectations.

Remember, the truth is that in this life, there is suffering. We face challenges with our health, issues at work, breakups, and death. For many of us, our pet friendships help us through the difficult times in our lives. Our animal friends can help us to decrease our suffering. That help might come in the form of physical, mental, or emotional support. It might just be companionship and having another critter around to receive our affection. Many of us will benefit from having our furry, feathered, or scaly friends nearby. We have a responsibility to take care of them, and to ease their suffering too.

When you learn about the Noble Truth of suffering, you also learn that the three poisons or the three unskillful roots of greed, hatred, and confusion or delusion are what lead us to experience clinging and aversion. Yes, when you have a difficult day, coming home to your pet will help you feel better. But there is a deeper level to the source of your suffering and a more beneficial way in which your pet will help you transcend your suffering. Behind the suffering that you are feeling, there is the real reason for your suffering. Something happened that you wished to avoid, or you did not get something you thought you wanted. You are experiencing clinging and aversion. Perhaps in front of your entire team, your boss began to discuss someone who has worked very hard and produced amazing results. Your boss began to announce that this person was being promoted. You started to stand up to acknowledge the promotion, but then you noticed that one of your colleagues was already standing, and your boss was smiling at her because she was the one receiving the promotion. You were disappointed because you really wanted that promotion, and you really believed you should receive that promotion. You were also embarrassed, and you hoped that nobody noticed you standing. Before you can accept the fact that you were not promoted, you will experience clinging and aversion. You wanted that promotion; you are angry that you did not get the promotion.

There is a cure, or an antidote, for each of the three poisons. For greed, the antidote is generosity. The cure for hatred is loving kindness, and for aversion, the remedy is wisdom. In caring for your animal companion, you are accessing the antidotes to the poisons that lead to your suffering. For you to be a guardian, a kind caretaker to the animals in your world, you must be generous. Offer your favorite animal friend your loving kindness, and as you share a life with your furry friend, you will encounter wisdom. In this way, your pets are an important part of your journey, helping to guide you toward spiritual transformation.

In closing, and with my two cats staring at me, I leave you with this quote from Jeff Foster: "Maybe meditation should be called sacred purring."

Bibliography

"ABOUT US - New Leash on Life," December 12, 2019. https://newleashonlife.org/about-us/, https://newleashonlife.org/about-us/.

Aeon. "What I Think about When I Say Goodbye to My Beloved Dying Pet | Aeon Essays." Accessed August 6, 2023. https://aeon.co/essays/what-i-think-about-when-i-say-goodbye-to-my-beloved-dying-pet.

Animal Legal Defense Fund. "How Animals Differ from Other Types of 'Property' Under the Law." Accessed August 6, 2023. https://aldf.org/article/how-animals-are-treated-differently-from-other-types-of-property-under-the-law/.

Apr 29, Denise Flaim Published:, 2021 | 3 Minutes Updated: Aug 27, and 2021. "Pug History: Origins of the Ancient, Wrinkly Companion Dog." American Kennel Club. Accessed August 6, 2023. https://www.akc.org/expert-advice/dog-breeds/pug-history-ancient-companion-origins/.

Basu, Lex. "The 11 Best Animal TV Shows of All Time." AZ Animals, December 3, 2021. https://a-z-animals.com/blog/the-11-best-animal-tv-shows-of-all-time/.

Big Think. "How China's Monkey King Changed Western Literature," September 20, 2021. https://bigthink.com/culture-religion/monkey-king-literature/.

Billingsley, Brooke. "How Much Does a Pet Bird Cost? 2023 Price Guide." Pet Keen, February 4, 2021. https://petkeen.com/bird-cost/.

"Buddhist Funeral Rites for Pets Gain Popularity in Thailand | Buddhistdoor." Accessed August 6, 2023.

https://www2.buddhistdoor.net/news/buddhist-funeral-rites-for-pets-gain-popularity-in-thailand#:~:text=In%20the%20Buddhist%20kingdom%20of%20Thailand%2C%20cremations%20for,reincarnating%20as%20higher%20beings%20in%20their%20next%20life.

"Buddhist Symbols | Animals & Mythical Creatures: Dragon, Lion." Accessed August 6, 2023. http://www.buddhistsymbols.org/animals.html.

Carver, L. F. "When Pets Are Family, the Benefits Extend into Society." The Conversation, January 6, 2019. http://theconversation.com/when-pets-are-family-the-benefits-extend-into-society-109179.

Center for Compassionate Leadership. "Steering Clear of Compassion Collapse," April 21, 2023. https://www.centerforcompassionateleadership.org/blog/steering-clear-of-compassion-collapse.

Colson, Bret. "Pet Custody 101: Who Gets the Pets in a Divorce?" Survive Divorce, March 25, 2019. https://www.survivedivorce.com/pet-custody-divorce.

Decker, Denise. "Chinese Pugs: History, Art, And More! | Kooky Pugs," December 19, 2020. https://kookypugs.com/chinese-pugs-history-art-and-more/.

Deleanu, Florin. "Buddhist 'Ethology' in the Pāli Canon: Between Symbol and Observation." *The Eastern Buddhist* 32, no. 2 (2000): 79–127.

Dhammo, Punna. "THE BUDDHIST COSMOS," n.d.

DigitalHubUSA. "Average Pet Parent Takes This Many Pictures of Their Pets Every Year." *Digitalhub US* (blog), August 26, 2022. https://swnsdigital.com/us/2022/08/average-pet-parent-takes-this-many-pictures-of-their-pets-every-year/.

editor, Don Chaddock, Inside CDCR. "Saving Dogs, Helping People." Inside CDCR, March 4, 2020. https://www.cdcr.ca.gov/insidecdcr/2020/03/04/saving-dogs-helping-people/.

Ellis-Petersen, Hannah. "'A Ticket to the next Life': The Lavish Buddhist Dog Funerals of Bangkok." *The Guardian*, May 24, 2018, sec. Cities.

https://www.theguardian.com/cities/2018/may/24/ticket-next-life-buddhist-dog-funerals-bangkok.

Gray, Elizabeth. "Top 20 Pet Spending Statistics To Know In 2023: How Much Do We Spend On Pets?" Pet Keen, February 21, 2022. https://petkeen.com/pet-spending-statistics/.

Hawkins, Roxanne D., Emma L. Hawkins, and Liesbeth Tip. "'I Can't Give Up When I Have Them to Care for': People's Experiences of Pets and Their Mental Health." *Anthrozoös* 34, no. 4 (July 4, 2021): 543–62. https://doi.org/10.1080/08927936.2021.1914434.

Heirman, Ann. "How to Deal with Dangerous and Annoying Animals: A Vinaya Perspective." *Religions* 10, no. 2 (February 2019): 113. https://doi.org/10.3390/rel10020113.

———. "What about Rats? Buddhist Disciplinary Guidelines on Rats: Daoxuan's Vinaya Commentaries." *Religions* 12, no. 7 (July 2021): 508. https://doi.org/10.3390/rel12070508.

Hells in Buddhism | Buddhism & Healing. "Hells in Buddhism," December 17, 2017. https://buddhism.redzambala.com/buddhism/philosophy/hells-in-buddhism.html.

https://www.facebook.com/onegreenplanet. "Help Make Sure Factory Farms Are Held Accountable for Leaving Animals to Die in Hurricane Florence." One Green Planet, October 1, 2018. https://www.onegreenplanet.org/news/factory-farms-held-accountable-leaving-animals-die-hurricane-florence/.

"IBISWorld - Industry Market Research, Reports, and Statistics." Accessed August 6, 2023. https://www.ibisworld.com/default.aspx.

IMDb. "Rin Tin Tin - Biography." Accessed August 6, 2023. https://www.imdb.com/name/nm0863833/bio/.

"Is the Monkey King the World's Most Popular Superhero? | British Council." Accessed August 6, 2023. https://www.britishcouncil.org/voices-magazine/monkey-king-worlds-most-popular-superhero.

"Jatakas as Valuable Source Of Information On Ancient India - GKToday." Accessed September 27, 2023. https://www.gktoday.in/jatakas-as-valuable-source-of-information-on-ancient-india/.

"*Journey to the West.*" In *Wikipedia*, July 29, 2023. https://en.wikipedia.org/w/index.php?title=Journey_to_the_West&oldid=1167716214.

"JSTOR: History of Religions, Vol. 40, No. 1 (Aug., 2000), Pp. 58-81." Accessed March 31, 2013. http://www.jstor.org/stable/3176513?&Search=yes&searchText=Gold&searchText=Purple&searchText=Robes&list=hide&searchUri=%2Faction%2FdoBasicSearch%3FQuery%3DRobes%2BPurple%2Band%2BGold%26acc%3Don%26wc%3Don%26fc%3Doff&prevSearch=&item=2&ttl=674&returnArticleService=showFullText.

Karp, Kate. "Help Clear the Shelters before the 4th." *Long Beach Post* (blog), June 23, 2023. https://lbpost.com/newsletter/help-clear-the-shelters-before-the-4th/.

Koca, Tuba Tulay, and Hilmi Ataseven. "What Is Hippotherapy? The Indications and Effectiveness of Hippotherapy." *Northern Clinics of Istanbul* 2, no. 3 (January 15, 2016): 247–52. https://doi.org/10.14744/nci.2016.71601.

Kraeutler, Tom. "How Much Does It Really Cost to Keep Freshwater Fish?" *The Money Pit* (blog), December 15, 2018. https://www.moneypit.com/how-much-does-it-really-cost-to-keep-freshwater-fish/.

"Kukkuripa's Dog and the Sacred Animals in Buddhism — Power Animals of Enlightened Deities and Their Meaning - Buddha Weekly: Buddhist Practices, Mindfulness, Meditation," February 6, 2023. https://buddhaweekly.com/kukkuripas-dog-and-the-sacred-animals-in-buddhism-power-animals-of-enlightened-deities-and-their-meaning/.

LaVoy, Erica. "The PETS Act and Beyond: A Critical Examination of the PETS Act and What the Future of Disaster Planning and Response for Animals Should Be." *Mitchell Hamline Law Journal of Public Policy and Practice* 40, no. 1 (January 1, 2019). https://open.mitchellhamline.edu/policypractice/vol40/iss1/4.

Levin, Jack, Arnold Arluke, and Leslie Irvine. "Are People More Disturbed by Dog or Human Suffering? Influence of Victim's Species and Age."

Society and Animals 25 (April 18, 2017). https://doi.org/10.1163/15685306-12341440.

Levine, Stephen. *Animal Sutras: Animal Spirit Stories.* Rhinebeck, New York: Monkfish Book Publishing Company, 2019.

"Los Angeles County Animal Care." Accessed August 6, 2023. https://animalcare.lacounty.gov/.

Magazine, Smithsonian, and Jacob Brogan. "The Real Reasons You Shouldn't Clone Your Dog." Smithsonian Magazine. Accessed August 6, 2023. https://www.smithsonianmag.com/science-nature/why-cloning-your-dog-so-wrong-180968550/.

"Man Takes Dying Dog for Final Walk around PA Neighborhood — and Neighbors Show out Big." Accessed August 6, 2023. https://www.yahoo.com/news/man-takes-dying-dog-final-140738368.html.

Marleys Mutts. "Pawsitive Change." Accessed August 6, 2023. https://www.marleysmutts.org/pawsitivechange.

Martin, Anthony. "How Americans Are Buried Their Pets In (2021 Survey)." Choice Mutual, March 22, 2021. https://choicemutual.com/blog/pet-burials-2021/.

Mcdermott, James P. "Animals and Humans in Early Buddhism." *Indo-Iranian Journal* 32, no. 4 (1989): 269–80.

Messenger, Stephen. "This Is The Very First Cat Video Posted To YouTube." The Dodo, November 1, 2014. https://www.thedodo.com/this-is-the-very-first-cat-vid-792883536.html.

Moffat, S. Emerson, FRI., Feb. 12, and 2021. "Buddha Throws a Party." Accessed August 6, 2023. https://www.austinchronicle.com/arts/2021-02-12/buddha-throws-a-party/.

Official Nara Travel Guide. "Todaiji Temple." Accessed August 6, 2023. https://www.visitnara.jp/venues/A00485/.

PEDIGREE®. "The Evolution of Pet Ownership." Accessed September 26, 2023. https://www.pedigree.com/dog-care-articles/evolution-pet-ownership.

"People Who Love Animals More Than People: Psychology Of Empathy | BetterHelp." Accessed August 6, 2023. https://www.betterhelp.com.

"Pet Ownership Statistics and Facts in 2023 – Forbes Advisor." Accessed August 6, 2023. https://www.forbes.com/advisor/pet-insurance/pet-ownership-statistics/.

Pet Urns & Pet Cremation Services | MD | VA | NC. "10 Things That Make Horse & Human Relationships So Unique | Agape," October 17, 2019. https://agapepetservices.com/make-horse-human-relationships-unique/.

"Pets Are Family: Survey | ConsumerAffairs®," June 1, 2023. https://www.consumeraffairs.com/pets/pets-are-family.html.

"Pets: Good Companions Or Not? – PatchPets," January 4, 2023. https://www.patchpets.com/pets-good-companions-or-not/.

Pons, Corina, and Corina Pons. "Dog Custody: Spain to Consider Pets' Welfare in Divorce Battles." *Reuters*, January 6, 2022, sec. Europe. https://www.reuters.com/world/europe/dog-custody-spain-consider-pets-welfare-divorce-battles-2022-01-05/.

Psych Central. "You, Your Cat, and Anxiety or Depression," May 13, 2019. https://psychcentral.com/health/your-cat-depression-anxiety.

Rep. Lantos, Tom [D-CA-12. "H.R.3858 - 109th Congress (2005-2006): Pets Evacuation and Transportation Standards Act of 2006." Legislation, October 6, 2006. 2005-09-22. http://www.congress.gov/bill/109th-congress/house-bill/3858.

"Resident Population in the United States in 2023, by Generation." Accessed August 6, 2023. https://www.insiderintelligence.com/charts/united-states-population-by-generation/.

"Sacred Texts: Buddhism." Accessed December 3, 2015. http://www.sacred-texts.com/bud/index.htm#jataka.

ScienceDaily. "Not-so-Guilty Pleasure: Viewing Cat Videos Boosts Energy, Positive Emotions." Accessed August 6, 2023. https://www.sciencedaily.com/releases/2015/06/150616093357.htm.

Shong, Molly De. "Lama Zopa on Caring for Your Animals - Lions Roar," September 15, 2008. https://www.lionsroar.com/lama-zopa-on-caring-for-animals/.

"Silents Are Golden: Animal Stars of the Silent Era | Classic Movie Hub Blog." Accessed August 6, 2023.

https://www.classicmoviehub.com/blog/silents-are-golden-animal-stars-of-the-silent-era/.

Simon, Tami, ed. *The Dharma of Dogs: Our Best Friends as Spiritual Teachers*. Boulder, CO: Sounds True, 2017.

Speyer, J. S. "Jatakamala or Garland of Birth Stories – 1. The Story of the Tigress." Accessed August 13, 2023. https://www.ancient-buddhist-texts.net/English-Texts/Garland-of-Birth-Stories/01-The-Story-of-the-Tigress.htm.

"States With The Most Spoiled Dogs 2023 – Forbes Advisor." Accessed August 6, 2023. https://www.forbes.com/advisor/pet-insurance/states-with-most-spoiled-dogs/.

Stewart, James. "Dharma Dogs: Can Animals Understand the Dharma? Textual and Ethnographic Considerations," n.d.

"Talk by Reiko Ohnuma at Stanford University - YouTube." Accessed August 6, 2023. https://www.youtube.com/watch?v=NRNNJACWZh4.

"The Bhikkhus' Rules: A Guide for Laypeople." Accessed February 2, 2016. http://www.accesstoinsight.org/lib/authors/ariyesako/layguide.html.

The Humane Society of the United States. "Livestock Disaster Preparedness." Accessed August 6, 2023. https://www.humanesociety.org/resources/livestock-disaster-preparedness.

"The Jataka Tales: Why They Remain Relevant for Adults and Children Both; All of the Buddhist Teachings Contained in Stories - Buddha Weekly: Buddhist Practices, Mindfulness, Meditation," April 28, 2018. https://buddhaweekly.com/the-jataka-tales-why-they-remain-relevant-for-adults-and-children-both-all-of-the-buddhist-teachings-contained-in-stories/.

"The Jataka, Vol. II: Book III. Tika-Nipāta: No. 267. Kakkaṭā-Jātaka." Accessed August 6, 2023. https://sacred-texts.com/bud/j2/j2120.htm.

"The Jataka, Vol. III: No. 308.: Javasakuṇa-Jātaka." Accessed October 2, 2023. https://sacred-texts.com/bud/j3/j3009.htm.

"The Jataka, Vol. III: No. 316.: Sasa-Jātaka." Accessed August 6, 2023. https://sacred-texts.com/bud/j3/j3017.htm.

"The Jataka, Vol. III: No. 324.: Cammasāṭaka-Jātaka." Accessed August 13, 2023. https://sacred-texts.com/bud/j3/j3025.htm.

"The Jataka, Vol. III: No. 357.: Laṭukika-Jātaka." Accessed August 6, 2023. https://sacred-texts.com/bud/j3/j3058.htm.

"The Jataka, Vol. III: No. 407.: Mahākapi-Jātaka." Accessed August 6, 2023. https://sacred-texts.com/bud/j3/j3108.htm.

"The Jataka, Volume I: Book I.--Ekanipāta: No. 15. Kharādiya-Jātaka." Accessed August 6, 2023. https://sacred-texts.com/bud/j1/j1018.htm.

"The Jataka, Volume I: Book I.--Ekanipāta: No. 21. Kuruṅga-Jātaka." Accessed August 6, 2023. https://sacred-texts.com/bud/j1/j1024.htm.

"The Jataka, Volume I: Book I.--Ekanipāta: No. 22. Kukkura-Jātaka." Accessed August 6, 2023. https://sacred-texts.com/bud/j1/j1025.htm.

"The Jataka, Volume I: Book I.--Ekanipāta: No. 32. Nacca-Jātaka." Accessed August 6, 2023. https://sacred-texts.com/bud/j1/j1035.htm.

"The Jataka, Volume I: Book I.--Ekanipāta: No. 42. Kapota-Jātaka." Accessed August 6, 2023. https://sacred-texts.com/bud/j1/j1045.htm.

"The Jataka, Volume I: Book I.--Ekanipāta: No. 57. Vānarinda-Jātaka." Accessed August 6, 2023. https://sacred-texts.com/bud/j1/j1060.htm.

"The Many Ways Animals Teach Us Love, Compassion and Empathy - Animal Bonds," June 4, 2022. https://animal-bonds.com/the-many-ways-animals-teach-us-love-compassion-and-empathy/.

"The Thirty-One Planes of Existence." Accessed August 6, 2023. https://www.accesstoinsight.org/ptf/dhamma/sagga/loka.html.

University of Central Florida News | UCF Today. "Pets Are Not People | University of Central Florida News," August 19, 2020. https://www.ucf.edu/news/pets-are-not-people-even-if-we-pretend-they-are/.

University, Southern Methodist. "Sociologist Confirms What Pet Parents Know: Pets Really Are Part of the Family." Accessed August 6, 2023. https://phys.org/news/2021-07-sociologist-pet-parents-pets-family.html.

Ventimiglia, Diana, ed. *The Karma of Cats: Spiritual Wisdom from Our Feline Friends: An Anthology.* Boulder, Colorado: Sounds True, 2019.

Vera Institute of Justice. "Who We Are." Accessed August 6, 2023. https://www.vera.org/who-we-are.

Vettese, Troy. "Want to Truly Have Empathy for Animals? Stop Owning Pets." *The Guardian*, February 4, 2023, sec. Opinion. https://www.theguardian.com/commentisfree/2023/feb/04/want-to-truly-have-empathy-for-animals-stop-owning-pets.

Viagen Pets. "Pet Cloning Process, Clone Your Dog, Cat Cloning, Dog Cloning." Accessed August 6, 2023. https://www.viagenpets.com/product/initiate-cloning/.

Wallace, M. A. "Sorry, But You're Not Your Dog's Mom." The Cut, October 27, 2016. https://www.thecut.com/2016/10/pets-are-not-children-so-stop-calling-them-that.html.

www.nar.realtor. "A Stunning Stat: There Are More American Households With Pets Than Children," March 13, 2023. https://www.nar.realtor/blogs/economists-outlook/a-stunning-stat-there-are-more-american-households-with-pets-than-children.

Yothment, Jacob. "How Much of the World's Data Is Cat Content?" Pure Storage Blog, July 8, 2023. https://blog.purestorage.com/perspectives/how-much-of-the-worlds-data-is-cat-content/.

Zahir, Mona. "Buddhism And Animal Ethics." Faunalytics, April 26, 2018. https://faunalytics.org/buddhism-animal-ethics/.

Zillow MediaRoom. "Gen Z Would Prioritize Pets over Partners and Kids If Buying a Home - Apr 11, 2023." Accessed August 6, 2023. https://zillow.mediaroom.com/2023-04-11-Gen-Z-would-prioritize-pets-over-partners-and-kids-if-buying-a-home.

www.ingramcontent.com/pod-product-compliance
Lightning Source LLC
Chambersburg PA
CBHW052138070526
44585CB00017B/1878